WITHDRAWN

# Contents

# Foreword

John Trimbur

A FEW YEARS AGO, I WAS DOING A WORKSHOP ON WRITING IN THE disciplines for a small group of colleagues. I asked them to read two short samples of student writing from an upper-division biology class. The first was quite well written, charming, but altogether un-academic in style. The second was also well written and, unlike the first, did a good job of capturing the measured tones and formal features you would expect in scientific writing. My point at the time, I suppose, was to use the samples as departure points to discuss what the people present valued in writing and what the particular disciplines take to be "good writing."

I asked my colleagues to give honest reactions to the writing, and two or three people said they liked the first piece more but knew the second was more appropriate to the occasion, when another of our group, a biologist who had been watching with a troubled look on her face, suddenly exclaimed she had been made to write *that* way (referring to the second piece) and so should her students. Her anger—and her sense of having been disciplined by powerful forces—was palpable. It hung in the air, as each of us thought back to our own experiences of learning to write in the academy, and what it feels like to enter a discipline and to go through the formative processes of professionalization.

To learn how to write—in particular to learn how to write and publish and survive in the academy—is (paraphrasing Wittgenstein pretty loosely) a matter not just of learning to obey a rule but also of learning a form of life. The problem, of course, as my colleague implied and as Gesa Kirsch's *Women Writing the Academy* makes clear, is that people inhabit these forms of life differently. "You approach from *one* side," Wittgenstein says, "and you know your way about; you approach the same place from another side and no longer know your way about."

Differences of age, race, gender, ethnicity, and class complicate considerably what is supposed to be a game that everyone starts at the same place. Without minimizing the influence of a range of social and cultural factors, Kirsch focuses on the effects of gender and the personal experiences of women writing in the academy. What I find so telling about her study is that once she gets her "subjects" talking (and because of the feminist research principles Kirsch uses, they sound like not so much objectified informants as speaking subjectivities), we hear stories that grow out of ambivalences toward academic life and practice that are similar to those my colleague articulated in our workshop—tales of the conflicting loyalties, everyday dilemmas, and contradictory feelings that go into the production of academic knowledge and the construction of individual careers in the academy.

The stories women tell about their lives writing in the academy are worth listening to in part because they challenge the conventional view of academic publication as a seamless meritocratic system that recognizes significant work, rewards talent, and ignores the rest. The academic genres—the article, the monograph, the scholarly book—supposedly offer intellectual communities effective means of communication; editors and peer reviewers a well-established set of criteria; and tenure and promotion committees a reliable measure for evaluating candidates' contributions to, and relative standing in, their fields. The problem, though, is women are less likely than their male counterparts to think of their work as sufficiently significant to write up and submit; women tend to hold on to work longer than men before sending it out; and women are less likely than men to revise and resubmit manuscripts that have been rejected. Kirsch's discussion of how writers struggle to establish authority in the academy helps us understand how and why participation in the meritocratic ranking machine is inevitably skewed and asymmetrical, not so much a matter of individual talent as a matter of social differences.

When women academics tell of their lives writing in the academy, we not only hear about the problem of equity and whether women have a fair chance to participate in the intellectual life of the academy. Their stories also call into question the genres in which academics write and the reasons they write in the first place. One of Kirsch's most striking findings is the desire, voiced by virtually all of her informants, to write for wider audiences, to transform academic work so that it speaks to the public as well as to other experts. Listening to the women Kirsch interviewed, one can discern the powerful personal investments that led these women into their respective fields of study and that have sustained them through the vicissitudes of a career in a world of old-boy networks. But the love of learning that comes across so strongly is most decidedly not a cloistered one. The desire to link research to broader audiences—to speak not only about, say, battered women but to and for them in order to affect public perception and policy—offers a view of knowledge that depends not just on its academic exchange value but on its social uses.

For me, this impulse to make academic work into socially useful knowledge is both powerful and revealing. It is powerful because it offers a way to rearticulate the relation between professionals and the public good by redefining the meaning of research and scholarship. And it is revealing because it suggests that the higher learning is not just about disciplining its practitioners, as my colleague's comment at the outset might indicate, but that the practitioners themselves, as Kirsch's informants have sought to do, can seize the academic tools of production for their own ends—to make the academy serve popular needs as well as certify individual careers.

# Acknowledgments

THANKS GOES TO ALL THE WOMEN WHO PARTICIPATED IN THIS study and gave freely of their time to talk with me. I would like to thank them for sharing their experiences with me and for their friendship, which has extended much beyond the scope of this study and has enriched my life in many ways. From them, I have learned more than I could have imagined; they have been important teachers for me.

I am grateful for a grant from the Research Foundation of the National Council of Teachers of English, which provided the funds for research assistance and transcription of interviews, and for a sabbatical leave and research grant from Wayne State University, which allowed me to bring this book to completion.

The research assistance of Zhuang-Zhong Lehmberg was invaluable in the initial phases of collecting data and conducting interviews. Many people provided valuable comments on drafts of the manuscript; specifically, I would like to thank Charles Cooper, Elizabeth Flynn, Peter Mortensen, Michael Pemberton, Joy Ritchie, Anthony Schreiner, the reviewers of the Studies in Writing and Rhetoric, and the series editor, Michael Spooner, for their feedback and support. Susan Richardson deserves special thanks for helping with final manuscript preparations.

Finally, I would like to thank close friends for years of friendship, conversation, and encouragement: Ann Bonner, Almira Karabeg, Laura Lang Matz, Krystoff Przykucki, Anthony Schreiner, Elizabeth Sims, and Patricia Sullivan.

# Introduction

THIS BOOK BRINGS TOGETHER TWO PROMINENT STRANDS OF scholarship in English: women's studies and composition studies. It is based on an extensive interview study that explores the academic context in which women in different disciplines and at different ranks write and publish their work. The study is framed by a discussion of scholarship on gender and writing, women's roles in institutions of higher education, theories of authority and audience, and the nature of academic writing.

Research in composition studies has only recently begun to explore the social and cultural contexts in which writing occurs. For example, scholars have begun to question models of composing that purport to speak about "expert" or "novice" writers, and they have argued that cultural, social, and gender differences define, to a large extent, who will be recognized as an expert in our culture, whose writing style will be regarded as authoritative, and who determines the discourse conventions that characterize successful disciplinary writing. Gender has emerged as one critical factor in these discussions of the social nature of writing.

Since women have not always had the authority to speak and write public discourse, establishing authority in written discourse is an important issue in women's writing experiences. This is particularly true for women in the academic setting because women have only recently begun to occupy the full spectrum of academic ranks across the disciplines, and because the university is an institution that serves an important function in the creation and dissemination of knowledge. Virginia Woolf's description of being denied physical access to a university library perhaps best illustrates the exclusionary practices of Western institutions of higher education (Woolf rendered this episode in a fictional setting so as not to offend the actual university "gatekeepers"). In a *A Room of One's Own* she writes:

> [H]ere I was actually at the door which leads into the library itself. I must have opened it, for instantly there issued, like a guardian angel barring the way with a flutter of black gown instead of white wings, a deprecating, silvery, kindly gentleman, who regretted in a low voice as he waved me back that ladies are only admitted to the library if accompanied by a Fellow of the college or furnished with a letter of introduction. (7–8)

Some seventy years later, women have achieved access to the university, but they are still not fully represented across the disciplines and across the ranks. Elizabeth Minnich, Jean O'Barr, and Rachel Rosenfeld caution us that although women in the past have "won a place for us in the academy . . . our presence is by no means reflected accurately, or adequately, at all levels, nor are all groups of women equally represented" (1).

Recent research in a variety of disciplines has begun to focus on women's roles and career patterns in the academy (e.g., Aisenberg and Harrington; Bernard; Simeone), their intellectual and educational development (e.g., Belenky, Clinchy, Goldberger, and Tarule), their moral development (e.g., Gilligan), the history of women's participation in education (e.g., Horowitz; Solomon), and their contributions to research and theory in a range of disciplines (e.g., DuBois, Kelly, Kennedy, Korsmeyer, and Robinson; Farnham). The study reported in this book contributes to this newly emerging body of work by investigating one particular aspect of women's experiences in the academic setting: their sense of audience and authority as writers of academic discourse. Scholars in women's studies have called for the study of specific conditions that shape women's daily lives in order to give credibility, authority, and value to their work and lived experiences. This study responds to that call by focusing on a particular group of writers (women students and faculty in five different academic disciplines at four stages of their careers) facing particular writing issues (their sense of audience and authority) in a particular setting (a large, urban university).

A host of gender-related questions emerge in this book. Studying women *across the disciplines* raises questions of gender distribution, educational access, and traditional and nontraditional fields of study for women; studying women *across student and faculty ranks* raises questions of women's educational development, career patterns, and hiring and promotion practices. Studying women *as writers* raises questions of gender and language, women's participation in public discourse, and women's "ways of writing." Obviously, the range of these issues is larger than any book can address, but my aim is more modest: to examine how the women I interviewed describe their research and writing experiences, to show the diversity and range of their scholarship, and to explore their ways of establishing authority and addressing audiences. The research questions asked in this study focus on women's interpretations of their writing experiences but do *not* try to document the current status of women in the university as reflected in hiring patterns, representations across disciplines and administrative positions, salary scales, or other trends. (For information on such trends, see, e.g., Chamberlain's *Women in Academe: Progress and Prospects* and Welch's *Women in Higher Education: Changes and Challenges.*) Research that addresses writers' interpretations of their experiences matters, I argue, because it can tell us how writers—women writers, in the case of this study—position themselves in the academic context, how they address and represent audiences, and how they negotiate and establish their authority in written discourse. I learned in the interviews, for example, that the difference between those women who described themselves as successful, confident writers and those who did not was often remarkably small.

Writing plays a central role in scholars' lives not only because the pressure to "publish or perish" exists in academic institutions but also because writing maintains and fosters a sense of community and defines a common intellectual enterprise. Linda Brodkey reminds us that the material resource of academia is written language: "In the academic community, networks 'exchange words,' rather than money or goods or services, because language is the coin of the realm" (*Academic Writing* 38). Perhaps nothing better illustrates the importance of writing in the lives of academic scholars than the first encounters I had with faculty and students I asked to participate in the study. Learning that the topic of my study was the writing experiences of faculty and students, participants usually had strong reactions; dismay, frustration, anger, and pleasure defined the spectrum of responses. One woman welcomed the opportunity to talk about and test ideas for her current book project (I became a useful sounding board); another woman suspected that I had been sent by the administration (I became, as she put it, her "conscience"); a third woman enjoyed reflecting on her publication experiences (I became the chronicler of her long writing career). Following feminist research principles (which call for, among other things, an interactive and open relationship between researcher and participants), I shared my interest in writing with the women I interviewed: being an assistant professor at the beginning of my career, I was curious to find out what I might encounter on the road ahead. Furthermore, since my doctoral research on experienced writers revealed that a range of social and cultural factors—such as past experiences with writing, personal histories, and a sense of self—all played important roles in writers' conceptions of others, of audiences, during their writing, I decided to pursue my interests further by focusing on one aspect that shapes writers' experience and sense of self: gender.

I begin the book by establishing the theoretical and historical context for this research. In chapter 1, I draw connections between two diverging literatures: the literature on women's roles in academic institutions (often presented without a discussion of issues in writing) and the literature on the nature of academic writing (often presented without a discussion of gender issues). In chapter 2, I lay out the design of the study and discuss the feminist principles that guide the research methodology. I also describe here the different backgrounds of participants (women students and faculty in five different disciplines—anthropology, education, history, nursing, and psychology) and discuss how I analyzed the interviews, what motivated my research questions, and what kind of relations I developed with participants in the study.

Chapter 3 examines how women in this study establish their authority in order to write and speak as successful students and professionals. I describe issues of authority in relation to academic rank, the use of disciplinary conventions, and the politics of publication. Chapter 4 addresses how writers construct representations of audiences and of themselves in their writing. I discuss findings in light of current theories on audience and academic discourse communities. I also describe the audiences many faculty and some students intended to reach: a public audience that extends beyond the academic circle of their discipline. In chapter 5, I examine how women's presence as scholars in the academy has changed the nature of research across the disciplines. As the title of this book—*Women Writing the Academy*—suggests, women are not only participating in but are also transforming the academy with their writing; in other words, they are redefining what it means to be a writer and researcher in the academic context. I discuss women's visions for future writing and research in their disciplines and describe the ways in which many have begun to transform the academy.

Chapter 6 points to a number of directions for future research and teaching. As is the case with any research that explores new territory, conclusions need to be drawn carefully, if at all. I raise questions more often than I provide answers in hopes of encouraging a multivocal dialogue among researchers, scholars, and teachers as they begin to address questions of gender, audience, and authority in the many kinds of writing emerging across the disciplines. Between the chapters are portraits of writers. These extensive, uninterrupted interview excerpts preserve women's voices, allow readers to reach their own conclusions, and avoid, as much as possible, the decontextualizing of quotes which is an inevitable part of the analysis presented in the chapters.

The material I gathered in the interviews is rich and provocative. I learned not only about women's writing experiences and their sense of audience and authority—the questions this study directly addresses—but also about the conditions of their daily work and lives. Successful writing demands extended periods of concentrated time, peace of mind, and a place to work. Tillie Olsen's *Silences* reminds us that women's roles as caregivers leave them with little leisure time, with even less uninterrupted, concentrated time, and with the habit of postponing their own needs until everyone else's have been met. Some seventy years after Virginia Woolf insisted on women's need for a room of their own, several women I interviewed, nontraditional graduate and undergraduate students in particular, have not yet attained that room of their own. During interviews, women talked about rising at five every morning and working late into the night in order to find undisturbed working time, about commuting long distances every morning and evening in order to maintain dual-career and long-distance relationships, about taking night classes during graduate school in order to hold full-time jobs. Women talked about reasons for interrupting their education: raising a family, supporting a spouse, or meeting financial obligations. Women also talked about early childhood encouragement to pursue their intellectual interests, about supportive spouses, and about establishing the time and space necessary to work and write with concentration. Read against this backdrop of their daily lives, the accomplishments of these women are impressive indeed: all are successful students and faculty, actively writing and publishing in their chosen fields. I hope that the many voices of women emerging in the interviews and inhabiting this book point to the complexity, contradictions, and possibilities of the lives of women writing in and across the disciplines. And I hope to convey some of the deep respect and admiration I developed for these women—respect and admiration for their work, their lives, their accomplishments, their aspirations and future visions.

# Women Writing the Academy

# 1

# Joining the Academy: Women's Roles, Writing, and Authority

THIS STUDY BEGINS WITH THE OBSERVATION THAT WOMEN'S ENtrance into the academy, particularly in tenure-track and tenured positions, is still a relatively new phenomenon. Being part of academic institutions—across a wide range of disciplines and at all the academic ranks—is still more the exception than the norm for most women. Women have been and are often still seen as "others" and "outsiders" in the academic context. This position of difference in the institutional and cultural context is likely to problematize academic discourse for many women writers. Scholars in a number of disciplines have begun to study women's place as "other" in cultural, social, political, and historical contexts. In literary studies, for example, scholars have explored specific instances of women's representations as "other" in literary forms of discourse, have reread and reinterpreted the canon, and have begun to restore and reclaim noncanonical literature written by or about women. Carolyn Heilbrun suggests that "we have come to recognize the degree to which the life of the mind is organized to reflect the politics of mind, particularly the politics of a wholly male-centered culture and university" (28). Heilbrun goes on to explain that "the life of the mind is a synonym for what is referred to as the universal—treated, revered, accepted as though it had been engraved somewhere as eternal and unchanging truth" (29). Feminist scholars have challenged such "universals truths" in almost all disciplines, noting that theories said to describe universal human values often reflect the cultural, ethnic, and gender biases of theorists (not universal norms). Kathy Ferguson suggests that "women in male humanist discourse have generally been among those others, consigned to the world of the acted-upon, of otherness colonized in the service of maintaining the sameness of the subject" (66). Research in women's studies has begun to focus on how the position of "other" affects women's educational development and career paths in academia.

## Women in Institutions of Higher Education Today

One important study that examines the career paths and choices of women faculty in higher education is reported by Nadya Aisenberg and Mona Harrington in *Women of Academe*. I review their work in detail because it is directly relevant to the findings of my study. The researchers conducted extensive interviews with more than sixty academic women across a range of disciplines and institutions, questioning women about their career patterns, research interests, publication histories, and personal lives. The women interviewed by Aisenberg and Harrington fall into two groups: women who pursued and succeeded with an academic research and teaching career, and those who, after an initial period of working in academia, were "deflected" and chose to pursue other careers. Aisenberg and Harrington expected to find large differences in the experiences and histories of these two groups of women but were surprised to find many similarities. They explain:

> [W]e were astonished to find less difference than commonality in the stories of tenured and deflected women. Tenure, in the academic world, is the point of security, a certain measure of success. On the surface it would seem that a wide gulf should separate the experience of those who succeeded and those who were either out of or on the edges of the profession. . . . What we found, however, was that the same themes recurred. Essentially, they are themes that depict an experience of professional marginality and of exclusion from the centers of professional authority. (xii)

Regardless of their degree of success within academia, most women remained uneasy with assuming roles of authority in their local and national communities. Even after years of successful teaching and publishing, many women still felt "inadequate, uncomfortable, [like] impostor[s]" (64) and had a "sense that their professional life [was] conditional" (67), temporary. Aisenberg and Harrington observed that for women faculty, establishing authority—in research, publication, and teaching—remained an issue of continued concern, ambivalence, and conflict, regardless of years of experience or academic rank. While men may also experience self-doubt about being in positions of authority, the critical difference lies in the fact that cultural definitions dissociate women from roles of authority. Aisenberg and Harrington point out that "needing constantly to prove your worth undermines self-confidence in even the strongest women" (67). They suggest two chief reasons to explain their findings. First, women have to break old norms, norms of silence, submissiveness, and deference in order to gain an "academic voice." That is, women have to assume roles and qualities traditionally associated with male behavior: assuming authority, displaying knowledge, arguing forcefully, debating with conviction, scrutinizing and criticizing other people's work (including that of men). Second, women tend to search for alternative approaches to research, teaching, and scholarship. Aisenberg and Harrington found that many women tried to develop alternative models of professional discourse, engaged in cross-disciplinary work, and preferred in-depth, private conversations over competitive, public debates. Yet, while many women attempted to define new models of discourse and searched for new ways of knowing, they were still being evaluated and judged by old standards. Aisenberg and Harrington suggest that "in deconstructing old systems of knowledge, [women] are undermining the foundations of their own training, and in reconstructing something new, they must name phenomena hitherto unnoticed" (81).

Women in the academic setting, then, are concerned with achieving two conflicting goals. The first goal is breaking traditional female norms (what Aisenberg and Harrington call the "marriage plot") and living according to traditional male norms (termed the "quest plot"). The second goal is challenging traditional approaches to research, scholarship, and teaching. Not only do women want to join the academy and succeed, but they are also simultaneously questioning and challenging the academic system in which they find themselves.

These conflicting goals can strain women's sense of confidence and authority and can leave a deeply internalized self-doubt. Aisenberg and Harrington conclude, "Women must struggle, consciously or unconsciously, to resolve contradictory norms and this struggle unavoidably compromises the development of the voice of authority that normally attends professional empowerment" (66).

Women students, despite their larger numbers on college campuses, still face many of the same issues as female faculty. Heilbrun, in her essay "The Politics of Mind," explains why women students, as a group, can find themselves in difficult positions in the academic setting:

> The woman student faces special problems. As likely as her male counterpart—perhaps likelier—to have mixed feelings about a female authority figure, she is at the same time eager to show herself worthy of the club she has been allowed to join. Deliberately or not, women are raised to be untroublesome, and to many women, young and old, it seems profoundly boorish to question the nice gentlemen who have let them into their university. (36)

Heilbrun's claim that women are raised to be untroublesome is borne out in studies that examine gender differences in teacher response and student participation throughout primary, secondary, and higher education. At the time of this writing, the American Association of University Women released a new report describing the many and serious disadvantages girls and women face at all levels of education (Kantrowitz, Wingert, and Houston). Myra and David Sadker, reviewing studies of primary and secondary education, found that teachers tend to give boys more time for participation in class discussions, ask them more challenging questions, pay more attention to their responses, and provide them with more extended explanations than girls (177). Moreover, Sadker and Sadker report that "boys are more likely to be praised for the intellectual quality of their ideas, while girls are more likely to receive praise for attractiveness of their work and general appearance" (179). The researchers conclude with the sobering observation that "although girls start out ahead of boys in most academic areas, as they progress through school their achievement as measured by standardized tests declines" (180). (See also Spender and Sarah, *Learning to Lose: Sexism and Education*.)

Women who achieve academic success despite these often unintentional sexist educational practices tend to be treated as *exceptional* students by both their teachers and their peers. That treatment, usually intended as encouragement and support, is deeply problematic: labeling a woman as exceptional still defines the norm for women as *unexceptional*. It places the achieving woman outside her gender group, thereby undermining the expectations held up for women as a group and sending that message to other women students. While male students may also be singled out as exceptional, one important difference lies in the fact that only women are praised for being able to "transcend" their gender. In other words, women who achieve academic success—as students, scholars, researchers, or teachers—are admired for being/acting unlike other women, a move that maintains cultural definitions of womanhood and achievement as contradictory categories.

In literary studies, exceptional women have even been praised for "writing like men." When a woman's writing received public recognition, it was often admired for containing male characteristics or qualities, while the writer's status as a "real" woman was questioned. Spender explains that "denying the real womanliness of a successful female writer has been one means of accommodating the contradiction [of successful female writers]. Even women who have been celebrated within the world of letters have frequently been singled out for their difference from other women" (*Man Made Language* 198–99). Joanna Russ has made a similar observation about the fate of women novelists who published their work under pseudonyms in the last century: when the writer's gender was unknown, her work was often praised, but as soon as the writer was identified as a woman, the standards for judging the work changed. Novels that once had received praise for their forcefulness and depiction of reality became subject to criticism for addressing topics deemed unsuitable for women writers (39–48). Such reversals of judgment suggest that written works were valued a priori according to gender: men's work was associated a priori with positive qualities and women's work a priori with negative qualities, a system Spender calls "plus and minus male" (*Man Made Language* 19). Suzanne Clark provides another example of this system at work: she notes that when men display emotion in their writing, their work is often called "passionate" (which carries positive connotations in literary criticism); when women do the same, their work is called "sentimental" (which carries negative connotations) (1–16).

To some extent, women have to become "men-like" in order to succeed as professionals, whether inside or outside the academy. Susan Chase has pointed out that professional women face a paradox: they often have to deny their gender in order to gain professional recognition, but once they do so, their cultural identity as "real" women is threatened (279–81). Julia Wood and Charles Conrad explain that "the term 'professional woman' contains the fundamental paradox and the potential double-bind faced by women in professions. There is a basic contradiction between abstract social definitions of 'woman' and normative behavioral expectations of 'professional' " (307). In other words, women do want to be recognized as women (not "iron-maids"), but they also want to be recognized as professionals and to dispel what are considered negative qualities of women (a show of emotions, for example). Thus, women in professional or academic settings occupy two contradictory cultural spaces: being a professional as well as a woman.

## Women in Institutions of Higher Education in the Past

Although access to higher education has been limited for women in past centuries (and in this century as well), it has neither kept women from seeking out an education nor from participating in public discourse. Outside the academy, women have long been active as readers, writers, and researchers. Anne Ruggles Gere, for example, has chronicled the development of women's clubs, independent reading and writing groups that were formed throughout the last century by women who wanted a forum for discussion, debate, and advanced learning. Some of these groups were modeled after the debate societies available to young men in colleges and universities but were organized and operated independently. Women determined their own reading and discussion agendas and met in each other's houses, in community centers, or their own clubhouses. They regularly engaged in research on a variety of subject matters and presented their work in formal essays or informal presentations to club members; some groups regularly sponsored lectures given by academic scholars and other experts. Furthermore, Gere reports that "club women frequently had little or no access to books, so they created their own libraries. In 1933 the American Library Association credited women's clubs with initiating 75 percent of the public libraries in the United States" (44).

Within the academy, women also have a long history of participation in the disciplines. Despite limited access, women have made important contributions to scholarship and research in different fields. Historians are just beginning to uncover and recover the important contributions that women have made to academic life and scholarship since the first universities opened their doors (e.g., Solomon). At times, women had to insist on or even fight for admission to institutions of higher education; at other times, women were encouraged to pursue their formal education, at least at the secondary level. Reasons for encouraging women to pursue an education varied from ideals of motherhood (the mother as conveyer and preserver of culture) to economic needs and a dearth of teachers. Educational opportunities made available to women in the United States in the last century were intended to reinforce existing cultural and social values, but they also had other consequences: women could earn a living, choose to remain unmarried, and gain social and physical mobility. Sally Schwager, in a survey of research on the history of women's education, discusses women's access to education in the 1830s.

> The academy experience, then, highlighted the central paradox in women's educational history—that education for women served the conservative function of preserving dominant cultural values of domesticity and subservience, while at the same time it provided women with the skills, the insights, and the desire to advance nontraditional values and, in some cases, even radical change. (164)

New opportunities for women in higher education, however, did not progress smoothly. In fact, new restrictions appeared as soon as larger numbers of women began to take advantage of educational opportunities. Schwager, reviewing a study by Joan Zimmerman of women at the end of the nineteenth century, observes that women students initially enjoyed access to all academic courses available to men, but progressively as their numbers increased and the feminization of the college came to be feared by the male leadership and outside observers, women were segregated into separate academic programs, separate housing units, separate social organizations, and were directed toward the women's professions. (184)

Only with the rise of women's colleges after the Civil War, Schwager explains, were women given the opportunity to "obtain intellectual training that did not assume a compensatory role for women scholars" (183). Women's colleges have played important roles in women's educational achievements and career developments, achievements that are currently being studied by historians and scholars in women's studies alike (e.g., Oates and Williamson; Rice and Hemmings; Tidball).

Despite their long history of participation in higher education, women rarely enjoyed the same opportunities as men to work as regular, full-time, tenure-track faculty members in universities. More typically, women held temporary appointments, often with large teaching assignments in lower-division courses that prevented them from pursuing research and publication to the same degree as their male counterparts. Schwager outlines some of the barriers faced by women who were seeking academic employment in the 1920s and 1930s:

> Even those universities that trained large numbers of women doctoral students usually refused to hire them as faculty. As old barriers against women's participation in academe were lowered . . . new hurdles such as antinepotism rules and the tenure track appeared that excluded women or confined them to certain fields, to the lower ranks, and to adjunct positions. By every measure, academic women were paid much less than academic men; their exclusion from professional and social organizations as well as their disproportionate share of teaching duties limited women's opportunities to pursue advanced research; and, not surprisingly, despite their greatly increased numbers and percentages in the 1920s and 1930s, women did not advance "normally" within their disciplines or institutions. Some saw this as evidence of women's lesser ability. (187)

Today, opportunities for women have increased, yet women still occupy a disproportionate number of temporary and part-time positions in institutions of higher education and continue to face greater obstacles in pursuing an academic career than do most men. Most women still assume primary roles as caregivers and homemakers, are more likely to postpone their education and career to meet family obligations, are more likely to assume a supportive role for their spouse, and are more likely to give up a job to follow a spouse or commute long distances between their job and a spouse's residence. These issues surfaced repeatedly in the interviews I conducted with women faculty and have been documented in a variety of studies (e.g., Aisenberg and Harrington; Simeone; Lie and O'Leary; Welch). Schwager cautions that "increased access to education [has] not resulted *as a matter of course* in women's intellectual, political, or social emancipation" (156; Schwager's emphasis).

## The Impact of Women's Scholarship across the Disciplines

Given the historic exclusion of women from participation in the academic enterprise, it is not surprising that women have had little input into the establishment of academic disciplines and institutions. Spender suggests that "it is the dominant group which has determined the ideas, the vocabularies, the images, and the beliefs; that has decreed and promulgated the ideologically sanctioned form of social relations. . . . Into this framework, women have been required to fit" (*Man Made Language* 199–200).

In a similar vein, Elizabeth Flynn observes that "men have chronicled our historical narratives and defined our fields of inquiry. Women's perspectives have been suppressed, silenced, marginalized, written out of what counts as authoritative knowledge. Difference is erased in a desire to universalize. Men become the standard against which women are judged" ("Composing as a Woman" 425). Access, then, is not the only issue at stake for women entering the academy. Women are also beginning to reexamine the traditions of their disciplines: the ways in which they have been taught to think, reason, and write. Feminist literary critics, for example, have suggested that the predominantly male canon of literature has taught women to "read like men" by identifying with male protagonists and seeing the world from a male perspective: "All women who have ever read a classic or undertaken an intellectual pursuit have imagined themselves as men. What alternative was there? Women in universities and outside of them have always 'read with a double consciousness—both as women and as the masculine reader they have been taught to be'" (Heilbrun 31). Only with the advent of the women's movement have scholars begun to reevaluate the canon, reread the work of women writers, and reexamine how men have portrayed women in their "great works" (see also Flynn and Schweickart; Fetterly).

Rereading the canon of primary texts is taking place not only in English studies but in almost every discipline across the academy. Scholars in history, anthropology, psychology, medicine, and the sciences are rereading the canons of disciplinary work to explore ways in which women's experiences have been omitted or distorted, to define new areas of research relevant to women, and to rediscover contributions made by women. In the process of questioning disciplinary traditions, women scholars are redefining what counts as scholarship, research, and knowledge in their fields. In their introduction to *Reconstructing the Academy*, Minnich, O'Barr, and Rosenfeld suggest:

> Having overcome some of the barriers to our [women's] physical presence, we are working now to be fully present, not by transforming ourselves but, rather, the academy—for the failures of education lie there. It was a great and noble struggle to achieve access; now, we must work to make the rooms we have entered suitable for all, not merely for the gentlemen of the club, and not only for the white ladies, either. If we would be fully present, we must all truly belong. (1)

Because women have largely been excluded from shaping disciplinary histories, feminist scholars are now engaging in at least three kinds of scholarship, according to Sandra Harding (3–5). The first kind of work is recuperative in nature; it recovers and reevaluates women's contributions to the disciplines. In English studies, for example, this kind of work has led to a reevaluation and reprinting of women's writing. The second kind of work focuses on ways in which women's exclusion from public life has led women to develop their own cultural artifacts and value systems. For example, much of women's writing in past centuries took the form of letters, diaries, journals, and autobiographies; these genres are now being reevaluated and restored to the literary canon. The third kind of work described by Harding focuses on reexamining the basic concepts and theories that define disciplinary work in order to uncover "blind spots" and neglected areas of research. For example, scholars in the social sciences are reexamining scholarship that purports to describe women's experiences, values, and development and have pointed to a range of women's experiences that have either been ignored or disparaged in past research (e.g., Lowe and Hubbard). Perhaps one of the most revealing—and disturbing—examples of this kind of research is Phyllis Chesler's work *Women and Madness*. Chesler traces the process of problem-definition used by psychologists in the 1950s and 1960s to justify electrical shock treatment and confinement of women to mental institutions.

All three kinds of feminist scholarship described by Harding have not only made important contributions to the disciplines but have *transformed* the nature of disciplinary work. DuBois and colleagues, surveying feminist scholarship in five different disciplines, argue:

> The cumulative effect of the feminist critiques of the disciplines was to establish incontrovertibly the existence and varieties of male bias in traditional academic inquiry. This bias, however inadvertent, accepts and perpetuates the ideology of female inferiority. Whether the particular discipline has almost completely neglected women—as in history or philosophy—or treated them as incidental to central issues of research—as in literature or anthropology—or considered gender as an important factor for research—as in education—feminist scholars have shown that the assumption that male behavior and experience are the norm for the entire human race is common to all. . . . The importance of these critiques reaches beyond the identification of male bias to suggest directions for subsequent research. Salutary critical examination of the fundamental assumptions of traditional scholarship has prepared the way for studies that yield a fresh, even revelatory understanding of women's being. (36–37)

Several academic women I interviewed in this study, particularly faculty members who had been active in their professions for decades, recounted how they discovered that their early research—based upon the training they had received in graduate school—was not "gender-neutral," as they had assumed, but "gender-blind."

One anthropology professor, for example, explained that she had to unlearn male-identified ways of reading, asking research questions, and identifying research topics. Once she began asking questions relevant to women's lives in the culture she studied, she discovered an area of research that had remained virtually untouched.

Not only do women, then, have to insist on access to the university and all its disciplines and ranks, but they also have to define a place for themselves where they can contribute to the ideas, vocabularies, research questions, and methodologies of different disciplines in ways that they find worthwhile and representative of their experiences. As more women are entering the academy across the full spectrum of disciplines and faculty ranks, they are beginning to transform the academy by developing new ways of conducting research, of writing and publishing, of teaching and interacting in their disciplinary communities.

## Questions of Essentialism

In an attempt to "correct" androcentric research, scholars in the social sciences and humanities are now focusing on women's experiences, identifying a range of new research topics, and developing new research methodologies and paradigms (e.g., Fonow and Cook; Spitzack and Carter). For example, scholars have studied "women's ways of knowing" (Belenky, Clinchy, Goldberger, and Tarule), have described women as speaking "in a different voice" (Gilligan), and have proposed alternative models of psychological and intellectual development for women. Some scholars have argued that there are essential differences in the development and values of men and women that can lead to different ways of thinking, setting priorities, making decisions, understanding relationships, and experiencing the world.

Whether gender differences emerging in this new research across the disciplines are due to learned cultural and social behavior or to some *essential* differences between the sexes is the issue of much current debate (e.g., Fuss, *Essentially Speaking*; Spelman, *Inessential Woman*; special issue of *Differences* devoted to essentialism with contributions by de Lauretis, Fuss, Irigaray, Schor, and others). Linda Alcoff calls this debate the "identity crisis in feminist theory" (257). She places cultural feminism on one side of the debate, defining it as "the ideology of a female nature or female essence reappropriated by feminists themselves in an effort to revalidate undervalued female attributes" (260). On the other side of the debate, she places poststructuralists who "reject the possibility of defining woman as such at all" (259) because any definition reinforces gender dichotomies and presumes the existence of a stable identity or subjectivity. The debate, then, centers around how to talk about similarities women share as a group without oversimplifying or totalizing women's experiences, a challenge I myself faced throughout this project when reporting on the experiences women described during interviews.

Scholars who argue that there are essential differences between men and women have provided an avenue for women to reevaluate their lives and find a sense of pride in qualities that have traditionally been undervalued or disparaged. Alcoff explains that "the cultural feminist reappraisal construes woman's passivity as her peacefulness, her sentimentality as her proclivity to nurture, her subjectiveness as her advanced self-awareness, and so forth" (259). The essentialist position has obvious benefits: it allows for a positive reassessment of women's attributes and contributions to society. But it also has drawbacks: it does not challenge gender as a social construct and fails to question gender dichotomies. Joy Ritchie summarizes the problem this way:

> For as women articulate and celebrate what is intrinsically "female," they risk coming full circle to the very psycho-biological determinism—the "essentialism"—that has circumscribed women for so long. When women make a claim for a unique and powerful female identity, they are left once again in a traditional binary, oppositional position: male versus female, power versus lack. (254)

An essentialist position can invert the gender hierarchy, describing the qualities and values of women as equal—if not superior—to men's, but it leaves intact a gendered and hierarchical system.

Poststructuralists want to unravel that gendered, hierarchical system. They perceive the essentialist position as a dangerous one and refuse to define the category "woman" altogether. Flynn summarizes the poststructuralist critique of essentialism:

[It] . . . depend[s], implicitly or explicitly, on a naive conception of female essence. Women, it would seem, have innate characteristics that transcend historical era, race, and class. Multiculturalists insist, though, that race and ethnicity make a difference, that a feminism based on the experiences of privileged white middle class women is unacceptably narrow and limited. Postmodernists insist that experience is always a construction and that individuals have no fixed identity, no stable identifiable subject position. ("Composing Difference" 2)

Yet, Flynn notes, feminist theorists cannot do without some notion of essentialism because otherwise the category "woman" becomes meaningless: "The problem here, of course, is that the category of woman ceases to have any meaning at all and so feminism is written off before its work of bringing about equality between the sexes and transforming society has been accomplished" ("Composing Difference" 3–4). Thus, not being able to talk about women as a group on some occasions in specific contexts denies the feminist project altogether. Flynn suggests that we need to theorize a space that allows us to talk about similarities across women's experiences but also leaves room for critical differences among women.

Feminist scholars, then, insist on theories that do not totalize women's experiences. In the past, totalizing theories of gender most often have reflected the cultural, ethnic, and gender biases of theorists and have been used to marginalize and silence people outside the dominant group (i.e., women, racial and ethnic minorities, and so on). I have collected quotes from four feminist scholars working in three different disciplines (political science, linguistics, and sociology) to illustrate the prominence of the call for multiple theories of gender. Kathleen Jones, a political scientist, suggests that "what is needed is the development of categories of analysis protean and inclusive enough to describe adequately the position of different women in different political systems" (26). Ferguson, another political scientist, describes her goal as "forc[ing] open a space within feminist discourses for greater acknowledgement of discontinuity, incompleteness, and tension. This effort to incite multiplicity against the somnolent hand of totalization need not weaken feminism as a strategy of political struggle; rather, it may multiply the levels of knowing and doing upon which resistance can act" (76). Alexandra Todd and Sue Fisher, two linguists, warn that "a unified theory for

gender and discourse is premature. . . . To develop a grand, inte-
grated theory too soon runs the risk of closing off new possibilities"
(12). And Jane Flax, a sociologist and psychoanalyst, explains that
"like other postmodernists I do not believe that there can ever be a
perfectly adequate, unified theory of the 'whole'. . . . But I do think
that theorists can provide more or less space for a variety of voices
and that they can be criticized for ignoring or repressing certain
questions that are germane to their own projects" (4–5). I concur
with these feminist scholars that we need to resist totalizing theories
when we talk about women's lives in order to allow for multiple and
changing perspectives; we need to refuse to define—and confine—
women's experiences to a limited set of categories.

The study reported in this book begins with the assumption that
gender is, in large measure, a socially and culturally constructed
category that shapes how women and men interpret their experiences. I assume that gender does contribute to—but does not determine—how women interpret their writing and research experiences. I do not argue for an essentialist position, one that holds that
there are gender-specific, essential differences in the way women
write and engage in research; rather, I assume that gender is a cultural construct that has a powerful effect on the interpretations of
our experiences, the mechanisms of which we are just beginning to
understand.

## Theories of Women's Intellectual Development

Important to this study is research that examines women's intellectual development because it focuses on gender-specific differences and challenges traditional theories of psychology and education. One such work is reported by Belenky, Clinchy, Goldberger,
and Tarule in the popular book *Women's Ways of Knowing*. I review
their findings in some detail because they bear directly on this
study. The researchers interviewed 135 women in a range of educational and public institutions (community colleges, research universities, family counseling clinics) in order to examine women's intellectual development and educational needs in early adulthood.
The study was prompted by a critique of the Perry scheme of intellectual development, a scheme derived from a study of an elite

group of young male students enrolled at Harvard. While the Perry scheme posits stages of development that eventually lead to commitment and membership in a community, Belenky and her colleagues found that "for women, confirmation and community are prerequisites rather than consequences of development" (194). The researchers found that while women were as capable of success as men in their academic pursuits, they often did not find their learning experiences meaningful. Lectures, debates, and formally reasoned arguments, for example, all reinforce what the researchers call "separate knowing," a form of learning that separates knowledge from the knower; that uses doubt to scrutinize the logic of claims; that denies intuition, empathy, and contextuality in favor of abstractness and so-called objectivity. The women that Belenky et al. interviewed, many of whom were high-achieving students at elite colleges, reported that they were capable of reasoning in the required abstract, objective mode and could excel in writing formally reasoned arguments but found these experiences divorced from their real concerns and life experiences. These successful women students concluded that arguments could be reduced to a game of rhetoric in which eloquence, not conviction, mattered; they learned to "criticize the reasoning of authorities" (107) but found that they needed to suppress their insights and emotions to an extent that turned arguments into meaningless games. In the end, rhetorical skills remained a public performance played according to teachers' rules and not according to the needs and desires of learners.

In contrast to "separate knowing," women preferred "connected knowing," a form of learning based on empathy, listening, and believing. Rather than building knowledge on doubt and the dissection of arguments, knowledge in the "connected" mode is built on trust and empathy. The women interviewed by Belenky and her colleagues preferred in-depth conversations with extended periods of listening and talking in an environment of trust over debates where turn-taking is competitive and speakers occupy antagonistic relationships. In short, they preferred collaboration and community over competition. Belenky et al. explain the differences between the two modes of learning and knowing: "Separate knowers learn through explicit formal instruction how to adopt a different lens. . . . Connected knowers learn through empathy. Both learn to get out from behind their own eyes and use a different lens, in one case the lens of a discipline, in the other the lens of another person" (115).

The work of Belenky et al. has been criticized, even dismissed, for being essentialist, but a closer reading of their work reveals that they argue for understanding gender differences as socially constructed. In an interview with Evelyn Ashton-Jones and Dene Thomas, Belenky herself comments that

> many people consider the four of us [Belenky, Clinchy, Goldberger and Tarule] "essentialists"—that is, they classify us with those who see sex differences as immutably rooted in biology. What we are really doing, though, is describing characteristics that women and men have developed in the context of a sexist and aggressive society, a society in which the public and private sphere of living have been drastically segregated. (284)

What makes Belenky et al.'s work—as well as that of Gilligan, who studied the moral development of women—provocative and invites an essentialist reading is the fact that the researchers uncover voices that have been unheard heretofore. They propose new interpretations of old research data and develop alternative models of human development. Their important contribution to women's studies, as I read it, is the challenge they pose to previously established norms, norms that were based on studies that either failed to include women as their subjects (e.g., Perry's study of young Harvard men) or described women's decision-making processes as inferior (e.g., Kohlberg's work on moral decision-making). In a very true sense, Belenky et al. conducted research *for* women (as opposed to research *about* or *on* women), a distinction a number of feminist scholars have begun to make (e.g., Harding). Kristin Langellier and Deanna Hall, for example, explain: "Research *for* women . . . does not simply generate new knowledge about women for the sake of knowledge, but conducts research with the purpose of empowering women (195). Belenky and her colleagues set out to empower women by listening to their stories, by taking them seriously, and by providing room for different women's voices to emerge in their book. Their work raises important questions about educational practices and gender: Are some teaching and learning styles more advantageous for one gender than the other? Are women at a disadvantage when asked to perform in debates and write argumentative essays?

## Gender and Language

Recent sociolinguistic work has identified a number of important differences in the conversational styles and language patterns men and women use in various social contexts (e.g., Coates; Lakoff; Spender; Tannen; Todd and Fisher). While examples of gender differences in language usage have been accumulating rapidly, there is little agreement among scholars on how to interpret such differences. In some of the early work on the topic, scholars argued that there are distinctly female speech patterns. For example, in *Language and Woman's Place*, Lakoff suggests that girls acquire female patterns of speech during their childhood socialization: "We find 'women's language' shows up in all levels of grammar of English. We find differences in the choice and frequency of lexical items; in the situations in which certain syntactic rules are performed; in intonational and other supersegmental patterns" (223). While Lakoff's work was groundbreaking at the time it appeared, it has since been subject to revision. Spender has criticized Lakoff's early work for implying that women's speech is peculiar if not inferior to that of men. She argues that differences in the speech of women and men lie not so much in the *actual* patterns of language use, but in gender-specific *interpretations* of language use. An identical word or phrase, for example, can be interpreted as an "absolute" if uttered by a man and as a "qualifier" if uttered by a woman, Spender suggests. She uses the sentence "Perhaps you have misinterpreted me" (*Man Made Language* 35) as an example, pointing out that the word *perhaps* can be interpreted either as a qualifier or an absolute, depending on the gender of the speaker. That is, a man uttering the sentence is likely to be understood as asserting his position; a woman uttering the sentence is likely to be understood as expressing hesitancy.

In recent years, feminist scholars have been reevaluating sociolinguistic research in order to highlight women's competence as language users rather than to point to differences or "deviances" that emerge when men's language is considered the norm. Pamela Fishman suggests speech patterns that have been interpreted as signs of women's greater insecurity and lack of self-confidence (such as a high use of tag questions and qualifiers) are actually "attempted solutions to problematics of conversation" (235). Fishman reinterprets women's conversational strategies not as signs of their subordinate social status but as signs of their successful problem-solving ability in different conversational contexts. Conversational analysis now often emphasizes the success of women's speech patterns: they are said to be cooperative, thereby enabling and sustaining conversations, in contrast to men's styles, which are said to be competitive, thereby leading to early closure of conversations. Coates reviews this recent trend:

> The most significant move [in scholarship] seems to be a reappraisal by women of the relative merit of co-operative as opposed to competitive strategies in conversation. Research carried out in this field suggests that men typically adopt a competitive style in conversation, treating their turn as a chance to overturn earlier speakers' contributions and to make their own point as forcibly as possible. Women, on the other hand, in conversation with other women, typically adopt a co-operative mode: they add to rather than demolish other speakers' contributions, they are supportive of others, they tend not to interrupt each other. (10–11)

The findings Coates reviews have important consequences for women: If women do indeed prefer a cooperative mode in conversation and, by extension, in writing, they may find some forms of academic discourse unsuitable for their purposes.

## Gender and Academic Writing

Feminist scholars argue that much academic writing reflects male forms/norms of discourse because it is based on notions of competition and winning, and it privileges formal, reasoned arguments. Olivia Frey, for example, studied articles published in the journal of the Modern Language Association (*PMLA*) between 1977 and 1985 and found that all but two articles written during that period relied on what she calls the "adversary method," a method that demands that writers criticize and attack other scholars' work in order to advance their own position (512). Jane Tompkins warns that verbal attacks directed at colleagues are similar in nature if not in kind to physical violence (as represented, for example, in the movie genre of Westerns):

Violence takes place in the conference rooms at scholarly meetings and in the pages of professional journals; and although it's not the same thing to savage a person's book as it is to kill them with a machine gun, I suspect that the nature of the feelings that motivate both acts is qualitatively the same. This bloodless kind of violence that takes place in our profession is not committed by other people; it's practiced at some time or other by virtually everyone. *Have gun, will travel* is just as fitting a theme for academic scholars as it was for Paladin. ("Fighting Words" 589)

In a similar vein, David Bleich suggests that "most academic discourse . . . loses its social bearings as it becomes ever more deeply immersed in the characteristically socially masculine value of competing and winning according to strict rules" (18). Bleich links the terms genre and gender, arguing that the mechanisms of gender inequality are reflected in the academic setting by a "genre inequality;" that is, one genre—the rational, persuasive argument—is privileged over all other genres. Such privileging perpetuates false dichotomies, limits the diversity and richness of writing, and impoverishes academic discourse and thought, Bleich concludes. Cynthia Caywood and Gillian Overing make a similar observation in their review of gender and writing pedagogy. They note that "certain forms of discourse and language are privileged [in the academy]: the expository essay is valued over the exploratory; the argumentative essay set above the autobiographical; the clear evocation of a thesis preferred to a more organic exploration of a topic; the impersonal, rational voice ranked more highly than the intimate, subjective one" (xii). Caywood and Overing argue that we need to unravel the system that perpetuates these genre dichotomies in order to teach and write the full range of possible genres.

All of this is not to say that academic writing is easier or more "natural" for men than for women. Obviously, men as well as women struggle with the production and reception of academic discourse, and it takes years to become comfortable with participating in professional conversations, speaking with authority, and reaching audiences successfully. Yet women who write academic discourse have a different point of departure than men: they first have to establish a place of authority before they can begin to speak and write with confidence. In establishing such a place, women have to challenge old norms and establish new ones; they have to create a space for themselves in an institution that has not always provided space for them. As Spender suggests,

> Writing may be a difficult task . . . but men writers do not confront the same range and depth of problems which women writers must overcome. Men have a right to write which women do not; they operate from a basis of shared subjectivity with publishers, editors and critics which women do not; they are encouraged and made confident which women are not; they have linguistic resources which enhance their image and support their values which women do not. (*Man Made Language* 201)

Furthermore, feminist scholars have pointed out that women's authority is easily undermined because they have to speak—and write—the "language of patriarchy," a language that places men in superior and women in subordinate positions in its vocabularies and representations of everyday phenomena and social relationships. In order to overcome patriarchal and sexist language, feminist scholars have called for developing a "woman made language," a language that would value (rather than devalue) women in their cultural and social contexts. Cheris Kramarae and Paula Treichler, for example, have developed a feminist dictionary, and Suzette Haden Elgin has developed an entirely new woman's language called Láadan in her fictional work *Native Tongue*. In the study reported in this book, I do not explore alternative uses of language (or ways of writing); instead, I focus on the writing practices of successful women faculty and students in five different disciplines. In other words, this study focuses on what writing in the academy currently is like for women, *not* on what it could be like; it examines the present state of affairs, *not* future visions. However, I do present women's goals for changing disciplinary discourse, and I describe ways in which they have already begun to do so in chapter 5.

Some scholars argue that the way to change the masculine, competitive values imbedded in academic discourse is to insist on teaching and writing personal essays (e.g., Bloom; Elbow, "Reflections"; Tedesco), and many first-year writing courses currently do focus on student narratives of personal experiences. But even if personal essays were taught exclusively in writing courses, the "genre inequality" described by Bleich would not be eliminated but only temporarily reversed. As students move into their disciplines, they would still be faced with writing academic arguments, only they would not have had the opportunity to practice doing so (see also Jarratt's argument for a review and critique of this perspective). I share Victoria Steinitz and Sandra Kantor's reservations

> about the wisdom of creating educational settings for women where critical debate, controversy, and advocacy are de-emphasized or, even more troubling, ruled out of bounds. We live in a world where power is distributed unequally, and those with access to money and power frame the terms of the debate. Women—poor, working-class, and women of color in particular—must learn how to unmask the prevailing views and figure out what's really at stake; we must develop the abilities to identify our own best interests and argue our positions as effectively as possible. (151)

More to the point, then, is an argument for the teaching of a wide range of genres in the many courses taught across the curriculum. When it comes to teaching arguments, approaches that deemphasize notions of competition and winning need to be explored. Catherine Lamb, among others, has taken up this task with engaging success. She draws on psychological and sociological notions of mediation and negotiation to define the goal of an argument not as winning but as achieving a negotiated point of view through cooperative dialogue. Lamb explains, "We need . . . to consider a feminist response to conflict, at the very least to recast the terms of the dichotomy so that 'argumentation' is opposed not to 'autobiography' but, perhaps, to 'mediation'" ("Beyond Argument" 13).

Most critics of academic discourse—men and women—call for richness and diversity in writing, not for an elimination of the prevailing forms of academic discourse. They ask us to write (in our academic publications) as well as to teach (our students) a multiplicity of genres; to acknowledge the importance of personal experience in all forms of discourse, including arguments; and to scrutinize the voice of disembodied authority embedded in academic discourse. Only now are we beginning to understand the gendered nature of academic discourse and its impact on scholars and students participating in the academic community.

# Portrait of a Writer:
# Professor Ashley
## "Walking between raindrops . . ."

Inserted between the chapters of this book are portraits of writers. By presenting extensive interview excerpts, I hope to create a rich picture of women's lives as faculty and students; as writers and researchers; as friends, mothers, and wives; as human beings with hopes, dreams, and goals for the future. The five portraits of writers (chosen from a total of thirty-five participants) represent the range of disciplines and academic ranks of the women interviewed for this study. I have provided no analysis in these portraits in order to allow women's voices to be heard, to allow readers to draw their own conclusions, and to avoid decontextualizing quotes as much as possible. Certain quotes from the interviews are repeated in the analysis presented in the chapters; here readers can find the full context in which the quotes occurred. Of course, interview excerpts capture only one moment in time; on another day, with another interviewer, or under different circumstances, writers might emphasize different experiences or express different views. I have edited interview transcripts only for readability (while trying to preserve the quality of spoken voices), arranged events in chronological order, and moved quotes referring to the same event next to each other. All writers' names are pseudonyms.

Professor Ashley is a full professor in anthropology, specializes in Middle Eastern studies, and has more than twenty-five years of experience in her field. She is a respected member of both her national and local community and has received a number of awards over the years. At the time of this interview, she had just returned from delivering a speech at an international conference. Professor Ashley speaks for a generation of women, many of whom were the first women to receive tenure in their departments and now can look back over several decades of struggle and achievement in their professional lives.

WHEN I FIRST CAME, WHICH WAS 1966, THERE DEFINITELY WERE problems for women, no doubt about it, getting tenure and all sorts of things. You could feel some of the negative attitudes in the department and in the university. I suppose it was a little surprising, but not much, because I felt it all the way through graduate school, too, where there were very few female graduate students and no female professors. So it wasn't a total surprise. I had additional problems with the area I was teaching in, the Arab Middle East, which has never been a very favorable topic in America. There are a lot of wrong opinions and prejudices; there were a lot of pressures on me for what I was saying and teaching. So the combination meant that there was quite a bit of pressure on me when I first came in. The seventies were good because by then, when I was going up for tenure, the women's movement had just started, and people were very aware of evaluating women. So that assisted me, I believe. I also felt that I had to write more and publish more than men to become tenured, especially in the area I was writing in. I was told that I'd better get a book out at first, whereas other people might not have had to [publish] a book. So I got my dissertation published.

I would say my mother was very important as a role model, to some extent. She was, I think, a feminist of sorts and pushed both of her daughters to do something with their lives. This was always behind me, always has been, still is. She still encourages me. She's eighty-six years old. She sends me articles on all sorts of stuff, so we've become very good friends. She reads a lot of things that I'm interested in. Another thing is, women in this department have supported me, women have helped each other here.

I got a lot of support from my husband, too. That's important. If he had not supported me, it would have been very difficult, both in the things I was writing and giving me time to write. He would help with the kids. I'm not sure I could have done it if he was not sympathetic and economically supportive. I was doing fieldwork, and even though I had some grants, you still need monetary support to get time to write. He's a professor, so he understands the need. It was very useful in my career to have a supportive husband—not that he did as much work as I did, but he did give a lot of help, where some men don't give any. He shared a lot of babysitting.

My writing has always been done at home. My children, it's hard just trying to squeeze them in. It's hard for women. Our concentration is always so interrupted because we have to think about so many other things. For women that's a real big disadvantage. It's hard to get big pieces of time to work without interruption; I think that leads to what men call "scatter brain." But we don't have wives to take care of kids, do the laundry. It's a real disadvantage for women, professionally—the writing. It does take concentration; you have to have time. I used to do a lot of it at night when I was younger; it's hard to do now. There would be times when I would stay up very late, writing until two o'clock.

All of the high points in my career just happened recently. A few weeks ago, I journeyed to Oxford to give a paper. I had my way and everything paid, and I was very happy about that. I had never seen Oxford, and it was just a very nice experience to be invited. So I spent a week there, and it was fun and very beneficial professionally. I met a lot of people. I had read their work but had never seen them. Another high point: I got an award. I've worked very much in the community, in the Arab community, and I got an award for this. That meant a lot to me professionally.

I try to make most of what I write at least usable to the community, as much as I can. I think we have to give back to the people we take information from, so I try to do that as much as I can. I don't get any brownie points academically for that, but it gives me the feeling that it's useful. I think there should be some more latitude with writing. In anthropology, we have a certain anthropological style, a methodology which we have to follow. You learn a lot of that from your mentors, from your professors. It's not always good; it depends on whom you're writing for. Now I'm trying to put a book together, editing it with somebody else. It's for practitioners. We're trying to get a different type of writing, so that it's not all these figures and numbers and anthropological jargon that nobody understands, because if you're a nurse or educator, then you should be able to understand this book. So this is what we're trying to do. I really try to reach people in the community, [although a lot of my writing] is for colleagues who are interested in the Middle East social structure.

I think it's necessary to try and write for somebody other than your colleagues. You write for your colleagues, for your promotion and tenure and all this business because you have to, because you have to do it for your vita. They count what journals you published in and how many. So there's a lot of pressure to do that at universities—too much. I feel a mission to communicate with a bigger group than the academic one. I try and write things in newspapers and other forums. Time is always a factor. There is pressure at the university; you have to be sure to get your articles done. I think having tenure and having a full professorship, I can ignore that somewhat, which I couldn't before. So that gives you a certain freedom to do what you want to, although there's still pressure. But I don't feel the tension I felt before. I feel freer; that has changed. I don't think what I'm doing is that different, but I feel easier about it. I don't feel nervous [anymore].

When you're trying to get up the ladder, especially getting tenure—that's the big one—you have to really have things in particular books and particular journals. I have published in mainline journals, too. You have to do both [academic and nonacademic writing]. I think I'm on both sides of the line. I am really doing both, which I have to do to keep a job. The interesting thing is, the material that you do for communities later will often benefit you academically in your field. People will know it, they will refer to it, they'll get to it. They don't get to it right away because it's not in *the* journal or whatever, but it does circulate back. It's helped me, too.

If I'm writing something academic, I think [my readers] will be supportive. If I write something for the newspapers, which I sometimes do, then I feel [readers] will be critical because of the nature of the research, because of prejudice. I guess I want to come across as an authority and give enough facts to back up my opinions. Maybe that's because I work in Middle Eastern studies. I feel defensive about that kind of writing; I think I have to defend myself in all sorts of ways. That's due to the nature of my subject. Sometimes I get cut off by political forces that don't like what I'm saying.

It's a very tricky area. It's like "walking between raindrops," as we say. It's a Middle Eastern saying, and often I feel like that's what

I'm doing. It's very frustrating to do that. It's been hard for Middle East scholars to get their materials published until very recently. I would say until probably 1980–82, it's been very difficult. In fact, Arabs went off and set up their own presses and met at their own conferences so that they could publish their own materials. No one would even accept that it's a topic. It was terrible. So they formed their own professional organization, and still, it's not easy. Although in the eighties it has become easier; there's been a proliferation.

I never really published in a moneymaking place, and I think that may have to do with being a female writer, quite honestly. I was pressured to publish as quickly as I could, to take whatever I could. My first books, I got no monetary benefit from them. One was academic and the other [one was published] by a nonprofit organization, so I really just didn't get anything off of either book. I always felt that if I had been a man, or somebody a little more secure, I would have sat around longer, waiting to find a better deal. Maybe I would have gotten a publisher where I would get some money. A lot of people said, "Why did you publish it with that agency and didn't get any money for it?" And one of the books went into a third printing; it was used a lot. The third printing [came out] twelve years after it was first published, so it really had sold. But I never thought of money.

I remember one thing, as far as women go. When our chair left, I remember her saying once, "Oh, I'm just so glad to be teaching. I'd teach for nothing." And she is a very famous person now, but this was early. She said, "This is such an honor to be able to teach," and I used to feel, not quite that way, but very similarly, that you were just so glad to have a job and be doing what you liked to do. Money was quite secondary. Of course, we both were married, so we weren't single people. We did have an alternative income. But I look back on that, and I think that is very much part of being a woman, as far as I can see. I don't think you would ever find a man saying that.

I've gotten involved in women's groups, Middle East women's studies organizations. In a sense, that's a subgroup in my area. The fact that you are a woman has a lot to do with what you see, how you see things when you go into the field. To some extent, since all my teachers were males, I probably initially adopted some of their attitudes. When I first went out to do field work, I was doing a lot of work that they thought was important, that I'd been taught to think was important. When I first went into anthropology, I was not really looking at women's issues. I was looking at what I had been taught to look at. I was looking at property relations and things like that.

In that sense, I guess I changed. Many women have shifted gears in writing, have looked at different things and felt freer to write about them. I think I have. Later, when women started writing about women, we were some of the earliest in anthropology, except for Margaret Mead. My mentor and myself and some other people got together and had a conference on women's roles in 1966. People were sort of amazed at this early conference, that we were just looking at women's roles and had a conference about it. It was one of the first conferences that ever happened. People thought, "Well, why are they doing this? Why would they separate out women and study them?" And I had to go back and draw things out of my materials because I hadn't focused on that. After that, I've been writing more on women's roles, and I still am.

So your gender has a lot to do with field research, with what you do, how you see things. As I said, I've changed, but I still appreciate a lot of what I learned. Now I've learned that women view things differently than men, and in a sense, you can get two views of reality. I've gotten more interested in women subjects, in their viewpoints. I ignored them initially because men have ignored them. That's what I was taught to do, so in a sense, I think I've become a better ethnographer, a better anthropologist. Coming out of the sixties, academia was still very dominated by men, even though we probably had more women than a lot of [other] fields. In the seventies, it started to crumble. I think it became a better field, with different viewpoints, and hopefully I'm a better anthropologist.

# 2

# The Study:
# Design, Method, and Assumptions

THE STUDY DESCRIBED IN THIS BOOK EXPLORES HOW WOMEN IN different disciplines perceive and describe their experiences as writers in the academic setting. Specifically, the study focuses on women's sense of audience and authority as they write professional discourse. I used multiple interviews with participants as my primary source of information and writing samples as a secondary source. The design of the study is informed by feminist principles of research that call into question such concepts as objectivity, validity, and reliability. Harding, for example, argues that a feminist approach to research includes an open discussion of (1) the researcher's relation with participants (the researcher's role and authority are never neutral), (2) the purpose of the researcher's questions (they must be grounded in and relevant to the participants' experiences), and (3) the researcher's agenda (it is never disinterested). Feminist researchers start with the premise that research methods are never neutral, impartial, or disinterested. They argue that researchers should acknowledge their research interests openly—to research participants and to readers of research reports—and they should involve participants in developing research questions. A researcher's self-aware stance can strengthen research studies, feminist scholars contend, because additional insights are gained when researchers and participants interact. Researchers will be less likely to ignore their own cultural, class, and gender biases, and their research designs will include conscious decision-making about what methods are used for what purpose and for whose benefit. (For further discussions of feminist methodology, see Fonow and Cook; Spitzack and Carter. For feminist methodology as it applies to composition research, see Flynn, "Composing 'Composing as a Woman' "; Kirsch, "Methodological Pluralism"; and Sullivan, "Feminism and Methodology.") The feminist research principles described by Harding informed the design of this study, as I discuss below. Although the subheadings of this chapter appear to indicate a rather traditional research report, the discussion within each section, the last section of this chapter, and the overall organization of the book (e.g., the portraits of writers between chapters) all indicate the extent to which this research is shaped by a feminist methodology.

## Design and Method

### Participants

Thirty-five women (twenty students and fifteen faculty members) in five different academic disciplines—anthropology, education, history, nursing, and psychology—participated in this study. These women represent four different ranks in the university: undergraduate and graduate students and faculty before and after tenure. I interviewed three faculty members and four students (two undergraduate, two graduate)—a total of seven women—from each discipline. I selected women who were regularly writing and publishing in their fields: students completing research reports, writing term papers, or working on theses for graduate degrees; faculty writing scholarly articles and books for publication, preparing presentations for national conferences, and participating regularly in local and national disciplinary forums.

The thirty-five participants represented a variety of ages and came from diverse backgrounds. A number of the students were nontraditional—that is, either they returned to the university after having interrupted their educations (to raise children, for example) or they enrolled in the university for the first time after having participated in the work force. Many of the students were also first-generation college students. All graduate students—seven doctoral and three master's students—were over twenty-six years of age; six were around forty. Of the ten undergraduate students, nine were of traditional college age (late teens and early twenties); only one was around forty.

The fifteen faculty members also represented diverse ages and backgrounds: many pursued academic careers while raising families, were in dual career (and commuting) relationships, or had pursued careers outside the university. Three faculty members had been nontraditional students themselves and had begun their academic careers late in life. The majority of women participating in the study were Caucasian; only one student was of African-American, and one faculty member of African-Caribbean, descent. Three women held dual academic ranks: two worked as full-time lecturers while completing their doctoral work, and one full professor had become a full-time administrator but continued to pursue her research actively.

Important to note is that all participants are successful writers and respected members of their communities. Thus, emerging in this book are portraits of women that are based on a highly selective population. I purposely chose this population to learn about the writing strategies of successful writers, their ways of establishing authority, and the kinds of audiences they address in different disciplinary settings. These portraits are not meant to be broadly representative; rather, they are meant to illustrate the diverse writing and research experiences of some academic women. This study does not examine potential obstacles that can discourage women from writing and from participating in the academy—obstacles such as writer's block, lack of confidence, or marginalization within the profession. Such issues have been investigated in other studies (e.g., Cayton has written about gender-specific features of writing block; Aisenberg and Harrington's study included women who decided to leave the academy; Simeone details the many different obstacles academic women face in their daily lives).

Disciplines Represented

Three criteria guided my selection of disciplines: (1) seven women—three faculty members and four students—had to be available in each discipline to participate in the study; (2) the faculty members from each discipline had to occupy positions across the assistant, associate, and full professor ranks; (3) the widest range of disciplines possible had to be represented. The first two criteria limited my choices considerably. While I had initially hoped to include a natural science as one of the disciplines I investigated, I found that women were either not spread evenly across these faculty ranks or they were overcommitted with professional responsibilities. Because so few women occupy higher faculty ranks (at the time of this study, only 9 percent of all full professors at the university where this research was conducted were women), those who do were frequently asked to serve on a host of departmental, university, and national committees and had too many professional responsibilities to participate in this study.

Given the limited choices I could make after meeting the first two criteria, I aimed for diversity among the disciplines. I included one discipline usually considered in the humanities: history; three disciplines belonging to the social sciences: anthropology, education, and psychology; and one discipline on the boundary between the social and medical sciences: nursing. These five disciplines varied in size, degree programs, gender distribution of faculty and students, and influence in the university setting as a whole. Anthropology was the smallest discipline with around twenty full-time faculty members; next in size came history, then psychology. Nursing and education both enjoyed the status of a college and both had their own administrations.

The range of research in which these women were engaged was much wider than the five disciplines might suggest. Faculty members' work often transcended disciplinary boundaries: one woman in education, whose background was in English, worked in interdisciplinary rhetoric (she is identified as a scholar in interdisciplinary rhetoric in later chapters); another faculty member had expanded her anthropological work to reach the business community; a third faculty member's work spanned history, economics, urban planning, and government policy. In fact, all faculty members described their work as interdisciplinary in some respect, a finding I discuss in chapter 5.

The Setting

All participants worked for or studied at the same large, urban university. The study was limited to one institution because institutional practices, such as publication expectations and degree requirements, can vary greatly from one institution to the next. Also, to be able to speak confidently about participants as a group and to describe their disciplinary community within the university setting, I decided to limit my observations to a single university. This university's student body is diverse in terms of race, age, and ethnicity: about 30 percent of undergraduate students belong to racial minorities, there are many nontraditional students, and the average age of the undergraduate is twenty-seven. Many students live at home, work part- or full-time jobs while pursuing their education, have childcare responsibilities, and commute to and from work and the university. The faculty body is also diverse in terms of ethnicity and gender distribution but is not as heterogeneous as the student body.

The metropolitan setting and the diverse student body distinguishes this university from other, more traditional institutions. Yet this university's population represents a pattern of varied student enrollment that is beginning to affect institutions of higher education across the country. In a sense, the participants in this study embody the characteristics that future populations of more traditional institutions will have. The students we describe today as nontraditional are likely to be the traditional students in the universities of tomorrow. The growing diversity of both the student and faculty population presents new challenges to curriculum development and academic career paths. This study, then, yields information about a population that will become more typical of academic institutions as they approach the twenty-first century.

The Interviews

Interviews have long been valued by ethnographers and reporters alike for providing direct, firsthand information, for allowing participants of a culture or an event to speak for themselves, and for providing investigators with an insider's perspective. But interviews also have a number of constraints: they formalize conversations, emphasize a question and answer format, imply a hierarchical relation between interviewer and interviewee (because the interviewer determines the issues to be discussed), position the interviewee as an object of examination, and can predetermine answers through the assumptions, categories, and word choices reflected in questions. Feminist scholars have called attention to these limitations of interviews and have argued for a critical examination of the interview process (e.g., Langellier and Hall; Nelson; Oakley). Ann Oakley observes that "interviewing is rather like marriage: everybody knows what it is, an awful lot of people do it, and yet behind each closed front door there is a world of secrets" (31). To reveal the "secrets" of interviewing and to allow for more open, less hierarchical interview procedures, scholars like Langellier and Hall advocate (1) using multiple interviews to develop a relationship of trust among interviewer and interviewee, (2) using interviews in group settings to generate genuine conversations, (3) having the interviewer share information about the purpose of the research with interviewees (instead of withholding it), (4) having the interviewer respond to questions from interviewees, and (5) designing questions that validate the experiences of interviewees (202–15).

When I planned and conducted the interviews, I took the feminist critique of interview methodology into consideration. I tried to eliminate hierarchical relationships with interviewees by locating myself, as much as possible, "on the same critical plane" (Harding 9) as the participants of the study (rather than studying "down" from a position of greater authority). That is, as a faculty member, I interviewed other faculty members, while a female doctoral student in English who assisted me with the research interviewed other students. We discussed the research agenda with participants, sought their feedback on topics not covered in our questions, and asked them to help us design additional interview questions.

The first interview focused on women's educational backgrounds, writing experiences, publishing histories, composing processes, and strategies for addressing readers and for presenting themselves in writing. Interview questions served as a guide for topics to be discussed, but we also let emerging conversations follow their own course. (Interview questions can be found in the appendix.) Furthermore, we answered participants' questions and shared our insights to allow a genuine dialogue to develop. The second interview focused on a recently or nearly completed piece of writing, its intended audience, its presentation or publication, and its development from conception through completion. The third interview—conducted with only six women because of time constraints—focused on themes that emerged in the two previous interviews. We provided participants with our preliminary interpretations of the interviews and asked them for clarifications, elaborations, and reinterpretations of the emerging findings. In other words, we entered into a cycle of conversation in which both interviewers and interviewees had access to, and could interpret, research data. Although we could not engage in these extended dialogues with all participants, the women we did interview a third time stated that our descriptions reflected their experiences to a large degree and that they had gained new insights into their own writing and research experiences through the interview process. Furthermore, I have continued to discuss my research with a number of the faculty on an ongoing, informal basis; the initial interviews set the stage for a number of valuable friendships. In that sense, this study aims to produce research *for* women, not just about women.

All interviews took place during the fall 1989 and spring 1990 semesters. The first interviews lasted between sixty and ninety minutes; the second, between thirty and forty-five minutes; and the third (for those who participated), around thirty minutes. Interviews were conducted in various places, most typically in faculty and graduate student offices or the research assistant's apartment, with only the interviewer and interviewee present. On two occasions, a young child or friend accompanied a participant.

Analysis of Interviews

All audio tapes of the more than seventy interviews were transcribed, amounting to 590 single-spaced pages of text. I analyzed the data by following the feminist principles for explicating interviews described by Nelson, who emphasizes active collaboration between interviewer and interviewee to allow participants to render experiences in their own words. The cycles of analysis consisted of listening to audio tapes repeatedly, reading transcripts, comparing transcripts and audio tapes, identifying thematic topics within and across interviews, comparing the identified themes with another reader (usually the research assistant working with me), and consulting with several participants about the importance they assigned to themes that were identified.

Assumptions

Conducting an interview study, I had to make a number of assumptions about the nature of information gathered in interviews and about the ability of interviewees to narrate and interpret their experiences.

## Self-representation in Interviews

Current poststructuralist discussions have problematized notions of authorship, subjectivity, agency, and self-representation. Poststructuralist scholars have proclaimed the "death of the author" (Barthes) and the "disappearance of the subject," arguing that notions of a "real self" are socially constructed concepts that are learned at an early age and that serve social and political ends. Poststructuralists warn us that as soon as we accept these categories as "natural," they escape conscious scrutiny and become all the more powerful. Alcoff reviews poststructuralist theories to point to their limitations:

> Disparate as [poststructuralist] writers are, their (one) common theme is that the . . . subject is not the locus of authorial intentions or natural attributes or even a privileged, separate consciousness. Lacan uses psychoanalysis, Derrida uses grammar, and Foucault uses the history of discourses all to attack and "deconstruct" our concept of the subject as having an essential identity and an authentic core that has been repressed by society. There is no essential core "natural" to us. (267)

The poststructuralist critique of the subject is important because it points to the socially constructed nature of the self, and it poses some fundamental epistemological questions for studies based on interviews. Interviews invite and encourage the production of self-representations because interviewees have to select events from a store of memories and make connections between disparate events to narrate their experiences coherently. This narration process is always an act of invention and improvisation: self-representations change as more questions probe interviewees' memories and provide room for new insights and revised narrations. Mary Bateson observes that "we . . . edit the past to make it more intelligible in cultural terms. As memories blur, we supply details from a pool of general knowledge. With every retelling, words that barely fit begin to seem more appropriate as the meaning slips and slides to fit the stereotype" (32). Participants often discussed their writing in terms of cultural commonplaces so as to compare their experiences with what they considered commonly known and true about writing. Several participants distinguished between their roles as writers, researchers, faculty members, students, and teachers, thereby producing portraits of multiple selves that were at times in conflict and at other times in accord with other roles. By talking about the participants' sense of themselves as writers, I am seemingly reporting on individual subjects with a distinct sense of self; at least I must report as if that sense of self is stable and identifiable. Such reporting can be an act of appropriation, of assertion, of power—an act that perpetuates the myth of the subject as it has long been dominant in Western culture. I do not resolve this conflict over the position of the subject in this book, but I do attend to the different and shifting self-representations that emerged in the interviews. (For examples, see the discussion of authority, self-representation, and narrative strategies in chapter 3.)

For writers, the poststructuralist critique of the subject raises a number of questions: If subjectivity is fluid and ever-changing, why do writers experience themselves as authors expressing intentions? Why do readers interpret texts as traces of authorial intentions? How can writers claim to discover their "real voices?" Susan Miller raises these questions:

> How is any writer capable of philosophical "seriousness" in the face of supposed free play among written signs or the persistent distance from intention we must account for in any writing? How can the writer, that is, make a statement when the inevitable juxtapositions of this statement against its many known and unknown allusions will capture and swallow the writer's "voice" and thoughts? And what guides the apparently self-contradictory wish to "make statements" in writing? (19)

Miller proposes that we "rescue" the writing subject by integrating postmodern theories with rhetorical theories and by developing a notion of the subject that is admittedly temporary, fluid, and shifting, yet at the same time manages to create the fiction of a stabilized self, a fiction we rely on in our everyday interactions with others. Miller's aim is to "renovate the writing subject, whose control of language is admittedly only provisional, but who is not a mere token in a language game" (20). She explains that "writers are neither entirely independent of nor dependent on systems of language. Their capacity to stabilize fluidity has to do with their abilities to be self-effacing in the service of a conviction that something may be *said* in a particular situation that will be *read* (both by this writer and by some reader) in no particular situation" (20; Miller's emphasis).

In a similar attempt to account for the subjectivity of writers in a postmodern age, Louise Wetherbee Phelps argues that we need to recover two concepts important to rhetorical theories: authorship and audience. Drawing on Bakhtin's notion of dialogism, Phelps explores the "disappearing boundary" between authorship and audience and proposes to use concepts like reader, writer, and text as heuristics, as a way to reestablish—at least provisionally—boundaries among different textual entities. Doing so allows us to "account for the fact that we do experience ourselves as authors . . . [that] we are not simply played passively by language and ideology, like a wind chime. To write, we actively seize, and just as actively reject, the signs and meanings of the semiotic winds in which we are immersed" (163). Critically important to both Miller's and Phelps's "rescue" of the subject is an understanding of the temporal, changing nature of discourse, of the importance of intertextuality, and of the necessary and unavoidable misreadings and rereadings embodied in all texts. But the shifting and temporary nature of authorship does not relieve writers of responsibility, Phelps contends. She ties authorship to responsibility and ethical choices (164), thereby anticipating feminist critiques of poststructuralism: that theory needs to be grounded in a commitment to action and change.

Feminist scholars have asked whether there can be a feminist political agenda without a notion of self that accounts for changes and motivates political action. While many feminist scholars welcome the poststructuralist critique of subjectivity, they are wary of theories that deny agency, change, and political action because such theories are likely to disempower women once again. (For further discussions of the relation between feminist theories and poststructuralism, see also Nancy Miller; Nicholson; Weedon.) Bella Brodzki and Celeste Schenck posit that "modern theory, of course, warns of the dangers of positing selfhood, indeed eulogizes and then celebrates the death of the author. But a feminist agenda cannot include further or repeated marginalization of female selfhood without betraying its own political program" (14). Feminist scholars want to reclaim subjectivity and agency, enriched by poststructuralist critiques, to enable social and political change. Alcoff, for example, advocates a feminist theory that begins with the poststructuralist notion of a socially constructed self but maintains the self as a site for political action, all the while recognizing the self as unstable, fluid, and shifting. She explains that "subjectivity can be reconstructed through the process of reflective practice" and that the "agency of the subject is made possible through this process of political interpretation" (277). Such a process of reflective practice emerged as an important theme in the lives of many of the women I interviewed; they embraced responsibility, political action, and ethical choices at the same time that they recognized the temporary and shifting nature of their subjectivity.

Narration in Interviews

Narrations produced by writers in interviews further problematize issues of subjectivity: they raise questions of veracity, validity, and reliability. By nature, interviews are densely textured layers of narration: writers narrate their experiences, an act that is shaped by interpretations of their writing experiences as well as by cultural commonplaces about what the act of writing entails. Writers' narrations themselves can change during successive interviews: being questioned about their writing experiences led some writers in this study to reexamine their assumptions and change their narrations during second and third interviews. Finally, as interviewer and interviewee establish a relationship, conversations become more candid, a common vocabulary is established, and the depth and length of conversations vary. The narrative layers of interviews are, of course, not limited to writers' descriptions of their experiences. As the interviewer, I too, have to narrate the interviews by choosing, selecting, and highlighting quotes from writers' statements as well as looking for patterns across writers' comments. The narrative of the research study is further shaped by my current interests, my readings of relevant literature, my understanding of related theories, my personal history, and my experience as a woman in the academy.

Such layers of narration are an inevitable part of all interview studies (though they are not always acknowledged), but they do not negate the importance of information revealed in interviews. What can be learned from examining the interview narratives of writers, for example, is how they interpret writing experiences and place them in the context of their lives. For the women I interviewed, these interpretations mattered because they shaped their sense of self, their sense of authority, and their sense of audience in writing—the very issues I set out to investigate. Brodkey reminds us that "one studies stories not because they are true or even because they are false, but for all the same reasons that people tell and listen to them, in order to . . . make sense of their lives: what they take into account and what they do not; what they consider worth contemplating and what they do not; what they are and are not willing to raise and discuss as problematic and unresolved in life" ("Writing Ethnographic Narratives" 47). Those same reasons motivate this research and, I believe, justify the analysis of interviews by women writing in and across the disciplines.

# Portrait of a Writer:
## Ms. Dannon
### "My life is in incomplete sentences.
### I don't have time for complete sentences."

Ms. Dannon is a graduate student in anthropology who returned to the university after practicing in the field of nursing for more than twenty years. She describes her adjustments to graduate school, her experiences as a returning student, her effort and struggle to learn to write academic papers, and her visions of changing the professional discourse of her field.

I'LL PROBABLY REMEMBER [GRADUATE SCHOOL FIVE YEARS FROM now] as being a lot of work but something that I really wanted to do. Nobody's making me do this. I'll remember the time and effort that I put in as an older student doing something I really wanted to do and going after that goal that I really wanted to go after. I'll remember some of the frustrations of graduate school, of using jargon terms, of jumping through the hoops. I think it's a good thing to be able to change professions or widen your horizons and build on whatever you're doing because that's what I'm doing. I haven't abandoned nursing; I just chose to do what I do in a different way, with different credentials, with a whole group of other people, which has made it better for me and better for health care in general, I think.

I have found the writing part of graduate school terrifying, terrifying as a woman. I think women, unless they're in an academic situation or in a school-type situation—where they teach or use writing skills all the time—in talking with other women that are in graduate school, I found that we don't use these skills, haven't been taught these skills in the same manner that maybe male students have been taught or required to use [them] in the professions they go into. Some of my problems with overcoming the terror of writing, or the failure or disappointment and humiliation of writing, come because I never learned how to do it correctly.

Before I got into graduate school, I thought things were adequate, I thought I was OK. Then I hit an all-time low in the first year of graduate school when I received such harsh criticism on my writing. I [had to learn to] separate that from personal criticism: "Are you criticizing my writing or are you criticizing me?" I think sometimes older graduate students, when they go back, have a hard time separating that. I survived it; other people quit. It made me totally insecure. It blew out everything that I had tried to do; one event took it all away.

Sometimes you find out the hard way by having your papers explode or having your study habits bomb. We survived because we're older and we kill ourselves to learn how to do it, but it would have been easier for us on the front end to have had some basic requirements. You as the student have to fill that gap. I don't think the university does anything for us in the transition part. I'm surviving fine now. But it was a very difficult way to go and a very discouraging experience—humiliating experience—to go through. It has taken me two years to get a handle on material to the point where now I know what I'm doing. But the two years have been very discouraging and frustrating.

And the other thing is, if you're a graduate student, an older person, you haven't done this in a long time. And it's hard to retrieve. So I think men, because of the professions they go into and the way some of them are tracked, just either use the [writing] skills more, or are in different classes that require them, or are in different professions that require them. So I think—and I don't think it's an antagonist feminist way of saying it—they got more [training] than I did. There was a division of labor. There *is* a division of labor. And not all of us have reaped the benefits of the overall expectations of being able to write and perform well.

The way I was socialized, in schools, young girls did certain things, boys did other things. We were tracked in different ways; we were tracked into certain professions. How I ended up in nursing and not medical school is definitely tracking. A lot of people my age are elementary-school teachers. They are not professors, older women professors; they teach kindergarten and first grade. A person my age married, and a lot of us put husbands through graduate school or medical school or whatever it was. And now that we're in our mid-forties, it's our time to do our thing. There [are] a lot of women, but many of us are still dealing with difficulties and adjustments which take away from our time and productivity. We're trying to deal with all the responsibilities that we have. For some reason, we have two jobs. I think a lot of us are dealing with home situations that take a lot of energy. Women who work all day do the same thing when they come home and have to clean the house at night, even though we do live with other people.

Sometimes a mother doesn't have a place of her own. Everything belongs to everybody else. And you close the door and sit in the bathroom and lock it; it's the only door with a lock in the house. But now I have my own room; I have a desk; I have a computer; I bought myself bookcases. Sometimes women don't have their own things if they are in a family situation. Everything belongs to the family, is a communal thing. But I have to claim my space. I bought myself a computer; I bought myself the gift of a computer. I got a [cash] gift from my father and instead of putting it in the family pot, I did my own thing and said, "I'm buying a computer. Everybody can use it, but it's mine."

The other thing is that when you write as a woman, you write your life. Your life is fragmented; you write fragmented. I write diaries, I write journals because my day is so broken up by other responsibilities as [the] wife and mother that I choose to be. I surely wasn't harassed into that, and I surely have enjoyed every bit of that. I'm not angry about that at all, but it has structured the way I think. I think in fragments. I think that's a reflection on how I write, how I think, and how I have to get through my day in general. My life is in incomplete sentences. I don't have time for complete sentences.

And when a woman has a project to do—my peers [and I] talk a lot about this—you don't have ten hours to sit down and write. You write in whatever time you can get. I do better in the quiet of the night or very, very early in the morning. I'm talking early, before the house starts going. When my children were home, I would get up at five and work five to seven before the energy in the house begins to change. But at night—it's just wonderful at night. It's quiet. I purposely control my environment or else there's just too much pulling at me.

It has taken me two years to learn how to read, let alone write, [in graduate school]. I can't even give you enough words to describe the disaster of my writing skills. Now I'm enjoying the struggle of learning how to do this, because now I see some reason for doing it. Maybe I created my own reasons, but I see some reasons that are meaningful to me. Until I made it my own, it just didn't make any sense to me because it's so repetitive and so wordy. But I appreciate the methodology now.

The types of writing that I have to do, they are primary source research papers; scholarly, documented papers. They are social science papers, just very technical, very wordy, very researched. I have never done this before, wasn't trained to do this. It's part of coming from another profession where you did the same thing but wrote in a different manner. It's the language that pulls together this profession and isolates everyone else from it. At first I thought it novel and unique, this type of writing, but now that I'm with the people in this other profession, I see it's all the same. The methodology they use is pretty universal, pretty rigid, which makes it unique to the profession. I think the papers are very much the same, just on different topics, different hypotheses, different conclusions.

I would like to come across in a very scholarly manner, I really would. I want to achieve that skill. At this point, my credibility rests with the material that I've researched, that I've cited; that's the only thing I have right now. I'm developing my vocabulary; I'm learning the vocabulary of the profession that I didn't know before, even things like the title. If you want to get cross-referenced in the social sciences indexes, there are certain ways you have to write your titles. I mean the creativity is taken out of things; you just better include big words or it doesn't work. All of this is really new to me.

Early on when I was using [technical] vocabulary, in one profession it meant one thing, and in another profession it meant another thing. So I would use it to mean one thing and then they would say, "What are you talking about here? That doesn't mean that here in this profession." Just basic words and concepts. Until I got a command of the vocabulary of the field that I'm in, I didn't have a command of anything. And the thing is, now that I do have a handle on it, and enjoy it, and am claiming the profession as my own, I see other people that are where I was two years ago and my heart goes out to them.

Now I'm putting out a product that's acceptable in my profession. But it puts me into a lot of avoidance behaviors, getting it down at the last minute. I'm so terrified to do it that I don't do it all along, and then I add the dimension of a time deadline to it, which just complicates the writing part. At the end, the finished product just kills me. I mean, I'm almost physically ill when it's finished.

But now that I'm learning how to do it, I'm getting affirmation from people who I feel are worth listening to. It's like a high. It takes me so long to get something out that's worthwhile, but then when I get it back, it's like, "I can do that." And there really is this amazing high that goes with it now. I have not mastered it yet, but I don't see it anymore as something I can't do. And the learning process has turned around because my attitude about it has turned around, to one of challenge versus one of just being beaten up and defeated all the time. It's feeling better. It doesn't feel good yet, but it's in control.

I had one professor, one professor especially has taught me the skills I needed in graduate school, empowered me to write, pushed me to a computer, listened to me when I was sad and when I was happy, treated me like a human being, also treated me like an adult, but with an understanding of the professor-graduate student relationship and not going over the lines. I've learned the material because she's turned me on to being able to learn the material. I'm not afraid anymore; I'm not afraid.

The professors that I had who saw through the mistakes to see what I wanted to say, those professors I'm not afraid of anymore. It's really kind of strange for someone my age to be afraid of something like this, but it is a stage of being judged by someone else. I think writing for me, writing is exposure. It's like being naked, and you can't fake it with a lot of things. When you write it down, you're pretty naked and you're alone. There's no one else there, and it's just you, raw meat. I mean you break into cold sweat when you hand it in, and then you kind of hope they're smiling when they give it back.

I'm not a confident writer. But I don't think that I lack the abilities to become one. I've gotten over that part. I just don't have the skills yet; I don't have the experience yet. The more I write, the better I get. I'm still terrified to write this dissertation. What am I going to do? What if I can't write it? But I'm getting better.

Now that I trust some people, I'll give them my work-in-progress. Whether it's the computer spellcheck or whether it's a real person. I do have some people that I would trust, that wouldn't judge me by mistakes that I made. The other thing I didn't realize is how much you rewrite. I really thought things came out that way, that people are brilliant. Then I talked to one of my best professors, who says he is criticized. One person trashes [his writing] and the other person thinks it's great. He told me how many times he has rewritten it. I had no idea; maybe other people ought to share more of that.

Sometimes, with work that I have admired, I have investigated the personality [of the writer] who put out the work. Sometimes they lacked in social skills or tolerance skills, or they isolated themselves. And the image was broken; I wanted the person to be a more rounded person. I've met a couple of people that are pretty balanced. I like to see a balance between scholarship and good human quality that makes you able to walk and talk and think at the same time. There are attributes that I admire in people; there are people that have characteristics that I think are worth modeling. I mean, I'm halfway through my life. I admire myself. There are attributes in myself that I think are worth sharing.

Now that women are going into anthropology, I think there has to be a modification through the way women write and see things— because the rules were set by British male scholars, and [they] only reflect British male scholarly writing. It's left out the other side of the world and the other half of the population. So I think that as women go into this field and learn to write in the good old-boy system, they'll begin to change the good old-boy system to a more holistic system. That is what I see, in the end, my purpose in doing this. Learn to do it their way, let them believe that I have credibility in the network, and then say what I have to say about possible improvement or addition to this particular methodology. That is how change ought to be done. But I think that one of the struggles is that women don't write this way. Women educated in a male system write this way. But women in general don't think this way. You

[have] to write that way, though, or you lose in the game, you never make it.

I think women think differently, write differently, express themselves differently, which is not a value judgment. It's just a different way of doing things. I think that as we begin to do this more and publish more about it, hopefully it will be accepted as another way of expressing oneself. I think that women, because of other things we do, have other ways of expressing things. One of my scientific friends discounted writing ethnographies as women's stories. And I said, "No. When you're doing an ethnography, that's people's stories. It's another way of telling about experience." But until there is some sharing of how things can be expressed, which may be a long way off, we're still going to be judged as poor writers—until men begin to read women writers, until they read the wonderful things that are put out by women. But we shouldn't have to go and put men's names on it, make our name "George Jones" to get somebody to read it and then come out of the closet later as a woman. But we do it differently. It's equally valid, but we're different. If it's all homogeneous, then it doesn't say anything. Diversity is how you reflect on what you are or what you are about.

# 3

# Working against Tradition: Establishing Authority in Writing

THIS CHAPTER ADDRESSES ONE OF THE RESEARCH QUESTIONS asked in this study: How do women faculty and students establish their own authority in writing and also address that of their readers? All writers have to establish their authority to write successfully and to establish credibility among readers. Disciplinary conventions play an important role in that process; knowing how to quote sources and how to locate one's argument in current debates, for example, enables writers to establish their authority as members of a disciplinary community. As composition scholars have noted, learning how to use disciplinary conventions can be challenging for writers. Brodkey observes that "learning to read and write academic prose is at once a matter of acquiring conventions, such as the procedures to citation, and learning when and how to apply them. That citation is a matter of some difficulty as well as importance can be seen most clearly, perhaps, in the writing of undergraduates" (*Academic Writing* 15). Not only is the process of learning how and when to use disciplinary conventions a difficult one, it is also one that involves compromise and negotiation. Patricia Bizzell, for example, has argued that learning to write academic discourse demands that students change their ways of thinking, reasoning, and understanding the world, a process that can call into question their values and cultural heritage (299). Along the same lines, David Bartholomae has noted that to succeed with their assignments, first-year students must imitate a voice of academic authority, often before they have acquired the requisite knowledge or experience (162). Writing with authority is not only a process that first-year students have to learn; it is a process that continues well into graduate education and professional life, as Carol Berkenkotter, Thomas Huckin, and John Ackerman have shown with their case study of a graduate student who had to change his ways of writing and reasoning to establish authority in his new discipline.

Scholars in women's studies have argued that establishing authority is further complicated for women—as well as for other groups historically marginalized in institutions like the university—because part of *having* authority entails being *perceived* as an authority. Since authority is usually attributed to, and exercised by, people who hold power in cultural, social, and political settings, and those people have been, at least historically and in Western culture, predominantly men of one class and race, it can be said that male voices have become closely associated—if not identified—with definitions of authority. Kathleen Jones suggests that our definition of authority itself may be androcentric, that if "the dichotomy between compassion and authority contributes to the association of the authoritative with a male voice, then the implication is that the segregation of women and the feminine from authority is internally connected to the concept of authority itself" ("On Authority" 152). Establishing authority in public forums, whether in writing or speaking, is an issue particularly critical for women because cultural definitions dissociate "woman" and "authority," thereby creating contradictory norms for women who occupy the cultural spaces of both "woman" and "authority figure" (also discussed in chapter 1).

We are just beginning to understand how issues of authority affect the writing experiences of women. Recently, several women academics have described the slow—and at times difficult—process whereby they learned to assert their own voices and speak with authority (e.g., Sommers; Tompkins, "Me and My Shadow"; Zawacki). Mary Cayton explains some of the reasons why establishing authority in academic writing can be problematic for women:

> For both women and men, engaging in academic discourse means *envisioning oneself* as having sufficient cultural authority to utilize a privileged language associated with authority. Moreover, it also entails experiencing oneself as *accepted by others* as possessing appropriate cultural authority. In some cases, it may also involve

a third component: grappling with the power relations inscribed in the discourse itself. All three of these factors can (and sometimes do) become problems for male writers. However, by virtue of their social positioning and long-standing exclusion from cultural authority, it is difficult for women to escape them. (323; emphasis added)

While women faculty and students *can* engage in traditional means of establishing authority—using disciplinary conventions in their writing, receiving appropriate academic credentials, participating in national disciplinary forums, and publishing in established journals—they *cannot* transcend gender as a category of difference in the way others perceive them in positions of authority.

The argument throughout this chapter, then, is that while learning to speak and write with authority is a demanding process for *all* writers—both men and women—gender is a factor that *highlights* or underscores issues of authority. My purpose here is to point to the critical intersection between gender and authority, not to determine whether or not certain strategies for establishing authority are gender-specific. In other words, women's reports of establishing authority in writing—their stories of compromise and loss, of negotiation and success—are a measure of how critical such strategies for establishing authority can become for all writers. I first discuss what women said about their sense of authority in relation to academic rank, years of experience, and the politics of publication, and I then turn to how they talked about being in positions of authority, how they narrated their intellectual lives as writers and researchers in the academy.

## Authority, Confidence, and Academic Rank

All writers I interviewed expressed concern about establishing their authority as scholars and writers, although the term "authority" was not always part of interviewees' vocabularies. Anecdotes about manuscript submissions, about seeking feedback on current and past work, about receiving editors' suggestions for revisions—and resistance to such revisions—all illustrate the central role authority plays in the writing of faculty and students alike. Generally, academic rank accounted for more similarities among writers than did disciplinary boundaries; that is, the more years of experience writers had, the more confidence they expressed in their writing ability and the more authority they assumed.

Senior faculty members with long publishing histories were least concerned with issues of authority. They reported relying on their previous research, publications, and reputations to establish their authority. They realized that not all members of a community are judged by the same standards, that not all texts are read with the same expectations. That is, established scholars are usually given more leeway with their writing—by readers, editors, and publishers—than less established scholars. Berkenkotter, paraphrasing Brannon and Knoblauch, points out that "readers grant writers authority on numerous grounds including professional achievement and recognized skill in discourse. The investment of authority gives writers considerable freedom with their texts, while at the same time insuring [*sic*] that readers will subordinate judgment to the task of comprehension" (319). In other words, well-known scholars typically have more liberty to make bold statements, draw conclusions, or argue for controversial positions than do younger scholars. A number of full professors I interviewed felt that they had more freedom to make strong claims than they did earlier in their careers:

I think having tenure and having a full professorship . . . gives you a certain freedom to do what you want, although there's still pressure. . . . I feel freer; that has changed. I don't think what I'm doing is that different, but I feel easier about it. I don't feel nervous [anymore]. (A full professor of anthropology)

Because we're both getting to be senior [the professor and a coeditor of a book], we don't have to prove ourselves anymore to people. You don't let the academic voice stand in the way [anymore]. (A full professor of psychology)

I just write significantly better than I ever did. I feel a greater sense of freedom now. My work is more difficult but I have the freedom to synthesize and be imaginative. (A full professor of education)

A writer's sense of authority was also linked to her level of confidence. Faculty members reported their confidence increased with the number of their publications and years in the profession:

> I am more confident than I used to be; I really think I write better now than I did fifteen years ago. (A full professor of history)

> I've gotten to be a better writer through the years, just by virtue of constantly tackling these increasingly more difficult projects. (A full professor of education)

> People tell me my writing is clear. I've gotten many compliments on my writing. It's lucid; it's persuasive; it's logical; it's coherent. I know, after writing now for over thirty years, that I know how to write. (A full professor of anthropology)

> I'm authoritative in the sense of what I know and what I think. I'm less confident and authoritative when it comes to expressing it. I will never be as good as I want to be at the writing process. (A full professor of psychology)

Most faculty members had grown more confident but also more humble over the years, a process perhaps typical of maturing writers. One full professor of anthropology said: "I used to be very arrogant about my writing and used to think I was a writer. Now I hope that I'm a writer . . . because I've read some fine writing over the course of my career in my discipline, some fine academic writing that much surpasses mine, and I yearn to achieve that standard."

Faculty members also recognized the importance of establishing their authority by adhering to the disciplinary conventions of their fields, such as making references to previous scholarship, situating their work in current discussions, highlighting their contributions to ongoing research, and following standard methodologies of their disciplines. (For further discussions of the role of these disciplinary conventions in academic discourse, see also Bazerman; Berkenkotter, Huckin, and Ackerman; MacDonald; Miller and Selzer.) Here are two faculty members' reflections on using disciplinary conventions:

You establish your authority by [following the format of] a research report; it has certain parts to it, and you do them well. There are certain criteria—for example, a good literature review. . . . So you're sure to do that, and then if you have a sufficient sample size, that gives you a certain amount of credibility. (An assistant professor of nursing)

I know a lot more about how to organize an article. I just have my little rules about the structure that I use. I usually write the method section first because it's the easiest. Then I try to write the results and the discussion so I know how the story turns out. Then I write the introduction to match the discussion and sometimes change the discussion to fit the introduction. (An associate professor of psychology)

Thus far, I have painted a picture of professional growth—of increased confidence and authority—for faculty. The factors faculty members discussed, such as years of writing experience, academic rank, and knowing how to use disciplinary conventions, are important for *all* writers' sense of authority, both men and women. In marked contrast to this picture of professional growth, however, is an undercurrent that can challenge women's authority: they cannot escape the possibility that others will fail to perceive them as authorities. While women can achieve all the credentials necessary to become "authorities in the field," there is always the chance that gender itself can undermine the authority of their work. Despite years of experience and academic rank, even women who were full professors expressed concern, at least some of the time, about establishing their authority. A full professor in history reflected on her experiences of gender and authority:

I've had years and years of experience and credentials, but the stereotypical reaction to a female never goes away. That pressure is so strong that I feel that I have to be super careful in what I write because otherwise the credentials will be questioned. . . . The whole apparatus of the scholarly world is such that people look at your output in highly critical terms, [asking], "Did she jump over all the hurdles? Did she make all the right references? Did she do all the right rituals?" You must not be too different;

you cannot state your ideas too boldly; you have to do a whole lot of dances. It damages writing badly. . . . As long as I'm in the academic world, [this pressure] keeps operating. It's obviously uncalled for and absolutely debilitating and harmful. . . . It's what takes away my energy, what keeps me from the full acceleration of my freedom as a writer, as a professional.

This professor raises two important points. First, she notes that "the stereotypical reaction to a female never goes away," that gender itself problematizes positions of authority for women. Second, she notes that compromise and loss can accompany the process of learning to use academic conventions ("it damages writing badly"); she alludes to what Ritchie calls the "problematic nature of the process of gaining authority by way of taking on the conventions and style of traditional academic writing" (Letter). Of course, all scholars have to engage in some "dances," as this professor calls the disciplinary conventions that signify membership within a profession, to build their professional credentials. But when women feel continued pressure to prove their abilities and establish their authority, the potential for compromise and loss becomes that much greater.

Other aspects of writers' cultural and social identities can compound this pressure, as a woman of African-Caribbean ancestry, a full professor of history, explained:

I don't think there's any question—when you're both a woman and a member of a minority, you don't have the same credibility as white males do. There's no question about it; it's a fact of life in this society. And you recognize it, and you try and cope with it, sometimes better than others. So I would say that for a great, great part of my career in this department—and I don't think it would have been any different in comparable institutions—I've been involved in building credibility. I think I have it now. I hope I do. It weighs heavily; it just affects a lot of things. It affects your ability to work, to sit down and discipline yourself; it colors a lot of your career.

This faculty member's observation—that a large amount of her time is spent building credibility—suggests that for women and other marginalized groups, the process of joining the academic commu-

nity and establishing authority is complicated by their cultural identities. Although full professors had been bestowed the external signs
of authority—academic degrees, promotions, and national awards—
they continued to feel the contingent nature of their authority.
Aisenberg and Harrington also found that for women faculty members, establishing a voice of authority remained an issue of continued concern, ambivalence, and conflict regardless of years of experience or academic rank. They suggest that "a major problem for
women, then, in developing a voice of authority, is that they encounter resistance to authority in women from the moment they
begin to claim it, thus inheriting self-doubt as an unwanted legacy
from the past" (66).

If gender and ethnicity are two factors that can make establishing
authority critical for women, the *kinds* of research women are likely
to engage in—research that originates from women's perspectives,
addresses women's concerns, and/or challenges male traditions—is
a third. (See chapter 5 for a discussion of the kinds of research
women in this study reported doing.) Simeone explains how challenges to women's authority can be magnified when their scholarship focuses on women's issues:

> Because research on women is perceived as being outside of the
> mainstream, biased, political, unimportant, and/or inaccurate,
> women whose interests and work lie in this area are at an obvious
> disadvantage in being published. This may be especially true if
> they challenge time-honored male-centered traditions and as-
> sumptions. The fact that much of this research reaches print
> through feminist publishers and journals further reinforces its im-
> age as political work on the fringes of scholarship, unable to meet
> the standards of its field. (71)

Not all scholarship by women focuses on women, not even the majority, but much of it calls into question the male traditions of past
research, and if it does so, it is subject to the same biases Simeone
describes. In other words, women who challenge disciplinary traditions—whether through a new methodology, subject matter, or research question—may have trouble finding appropriate sources for
publication and gaining the recognition necessary to establish their
authority as members of the academy. One professor of history ex-

plained the difficulty establishing authority in interdisciplinary work: "Each discipline . . . has its own ritual and its own paradox. And you have to do the ritual [of citation, quotation, and so on] vis-à-vis each discipline, and each discipline is different. The problem of amalgamating them is enormous. The minute you bring them all together, you have rocked the boat, and it's there where the problem of being accepted comes in." Because the majority of faculty members interviewed in this study reported transforming disciplinary research and writing in some form or other (discussed in chapter 5), they faced additional challenges to their authority.

All of this is not to say that establishing authority in academic discourse is particularly easy for men; their writing can be rejected, just as their authority can be questioned. What I am suggesting is that because a woman's sense of authority is more easily questioned than a man's—because she occupies a marginal position in the dominant culture and its institutions—a woman's writing experiences *magnify or highlight* issues of authority that concern all writers.

Students

Since graduate and undergraduate students typically regarded their professors as the primary audience for their writing (discussed in chapter 4), they reported having little authority over their writing. That is, they identified closely with the student role—the learner—who has to write for the teacher—the expert—to prove that she has understood the course material. In general, students who were older and further along in the educational process expressed the most confidence and authority. For example, a graduate student in nursing said: "My confidence as a writer depends on the topic. It depends on the subject, depends on what I know about it. So if I spend a lot of time on it, I feel more confident because I know how much time I spent. I know what I've read, that I understand it." Both graduate and undergraduate students placed the main source of their authority in the research materials they quoted, not in themselves or in their writing:

At this point, my credibility rests *with the material* that I've researched, that I've cited; that's the only thing I have right now. I'm developing my vocabulary; I'm learning the vocabulary of the profession that I didn't know before. (A graduate student in anthropology)

In the research paper, I just try to be real analytical, professional, use big words. I establish my authority by *paraphrasing, using direct quotes*, and then analyzing material. My reference page shows I [have] used these people's writing; that's where my information came from. Other than that, I really don't think I have too much authority until I graduate. I feel like an undergraduate student. That's what I am right now. (An undergraduate student in nursing)

I think authority comes through in a *clear presentation of the material*, in letting the reader know that you have a good acquaintance with the subject matter and with the resources, the available research. If I'm writing a paper and [am] able to cite five authorities on a fairly obscure aspect, that says I've done some work. That's the authority. (A graduate student in history)

Clearly, these students were aware of the importance of citation as a convention of academic writing. Since such conventions can be learned, and students wanted to demonstrate their competence as learners to receive good grades, they concentrated on this aspect of establishing their authority—at least they discussed this aspect during the interviews. Students did not discuss how they saw themselves or how they were perceived by others in roles of authority, most likely because they did not see themselves as possessing authority as writers or as makers of knowledge. It is also possible that because women now constitute the majority of undergraduate students, questions of authority are less visible—though by no means less important—during undergraduate education. Furthermore, women may not recognize and question the male traditions of their disciplines until they become deeply immersed in their fields of study, enter graduate school, major in male-dominated fields, or pursue academic career paths.

Only occasionally were students as committed as faculty to their work and to expressing their views. A returning graduate student in history remembered her confidence as an older student even during her undergraduate years:

One of my first classes was an English class. The instructor didn't like my first paper. He gave me a C. I went up there and said, "This is not a C; this is an A." So he gave me an A. He saw it my way because I know what good writing is. That's one thing I know—what good writing is. The man was ignorant; he understood that by the time I was through. That's one thing about coming back as an older student. It's very hard to get anything by me.

This student's courage to confront her instructor was unusual among the students interviewed for this study. Most students—both graduate and undergraduate—tried to establish their authority by making it clear to readers that they knew their research materials well.

## Authority, Ownership, and the Politics of Publication

Authority becomes a critical factor in the politics of publication. In having work reviewed, edited, and published, authors and editors engage in a complex process of negotiation: they debate what constitutes exemplary work, what kind of research is deemed valuable, what constitutes new knowledge, and what work makes important contributions to a discipline. Furthermore, authors compete for publication space in prestigious journals while editors compete for manuscripts from prominent authors. The politics of publication are powerful: they shape the history of academic disciplines and affect every facet of academic life—the nature of research, the institutional merit and reward systems, the availability of funds, and ultimately, the economic and political interests of institutions as expressed in their relations with government and industry. (For further discussions of the politics of publication and institutional histories, see Berlin; Brodkey, *Academic Writing as Social Practice*; Bullock and Trimbur; Graff; Herron.)

For women, the politics of publication are particularly critical because the academic community enjoys great autonomy and has a "long history of self-governance, of controlling membership by publishing work it finds scholarly and rejecting work it does not" (Brodkey, *Academic Writing* 14). Women cannot take for granted the same authority that is assigned to men in the production of discourse. Spender explains:

That males have determined the criteria of what constitutes good writing, that they have then also controlled the means of making decisions about what good writing gets published and what does not, and that they have also had the power to rank published writing, making or breaking the reputation of women writers, means that there is a virtual labyrinth which women writers must attempt to find their way through if they are to gain any stature in the culture. (*Man Made Language* 200)

Women in this study described a range of complex negotiations with coauthors, journal editors, and book publishers as their manuscripts entered the publication process. These negotiations shaped women's sense of authority and ownership in important ways, charted the future directions of their research, and determined their scholarly ambitions and goals. Their experiences speak of compromise and loss as well as of defiance and success. An associate professor of nursing described one of her publication experiences:

The negotiating process with an editor can be enormously difficult and demoralizing. I had one article where the editor and I spent hours on the phone arguing, discussing whether certain phrases should be in there. That is an issue, but it's part of writing for publication. It comes with the territory. One has to accept that there is a lot of ownership that you give up. You take a certain amount of risk. . . . But for the most part, I think that the editorial process is helpful.

Like this professor of nursing, the faculty members I interviewed realized that publication entails negotiation and revision, a process they found helpful in most cases.

One important factor that influenced faculty members' willingness to accommodate editors' requests for revisions was their position on the tenure track. Prior to receiving tenure, faculty members were more likely to feel pressure to publish and more willing to accommodate editors' and reviewers' requests—or demands—for revisions. A psychology professor described a difficult decision she had to make in negotiating the revision of an article she published prior to receiving tenure:

There was one case in particular when the editor essentially told me to withdraw half my data, because it basically didn't agree with her position. I really had to think about whether that was ethical, whether I was comfortable with that. The compromise that I made for myself was that I put the data into a footnote so that it appeared in the article but wasn't part of the text. I needed the publication [for tenure], so I did it. But I still think it was inappropriate, that it ended up being the editor's paper and not mine. But I compromised. . . . In general, I feel that the review process is a fair one, and except for this one instance, my papers have really improved as a result of the process.

Faculty members with tenure had more latitude to resist compromises, as this full professor in psychology, herself an editor of a journal, explained:

[Once] I had a terrible editor who wasn't just changing syntax and word choice but was changing meanings. And I wrote back a long letter and got an apology from the editors of the book. They restored virtually everything we asked them to. I have a very clear view that the editor's role is to catch inaccuracies, even in reasoning, and [to] help authors look as good as they can. And beyond that you stay out. You don't say things your favorite way; you let authors say it their favorite way.

But even one's rank did not guarantee ownership or full control of one's text. A full professor of history reported how a book chapter she wrote had been changed by the editors:

The editors chopped down my chapter themselves instead of sending it to me to be chopped, and so the style of writing ended up being theirs. I sent back quite an annoyed letter stating that in the process of cutting down, they had brutalized the writing, changed the subtleties, introduced outright inaccuracies by sifting what I had to say through their own mentality, and shifted my documentation around so that it didn't match what they had produced. I was quite upset by it. I protested and there was some modification, but only about one fifth of what I would have prepared.

At times faculty members resisted compromises with editors and changed journals or publishing houses to retain what they considered the essence of their work:

> One publisher did seriously entertain [publishing my] book but wanted a very different, more traditional philosophical study. Even though I very much wanted my work published by [that] publisher, I realized I wanted to write this book my way. And fortunately [another] press took it, and the only revisions they asked for were trimming down rather than changing content. So I feel an enormous sense of satisfaction that I wrote the book I wanted to write. (A full professor of education)

> Once I withdrew a long review essay from a journal. The editor changed it massively. Those weren't just minor editorial changes but major revisions. I wrote to the editor and said, "Sorry, this is mine; it is me. You will either reconsider the essay in its original form or return it." They wouldn't [reconsider it], so I published it elsewhere. Now that's a risk I'll take because I do not mean to go down on paper as anyone else. (An assistant professor of history)

As these stories of compromise and negotiation suggest, the politics of publication cut to the heart of establishing authority; women often had to decide the degree to which they were willing to revise their writing—and their ideas—to be published. Of course, all faculty—regardless of gender—encounter the politics of publication at some point in their careers, and they must decide whether to compromise and what kinds of compromises they are willing to make. For women the pressure to compromise can be compounded, particularly if they aim to transform academic writing and research. An associate professor of nursing, who participated in this study, reflected on her goal to include feminist views in her writing and on the compromises she had made in previous publications:

> I have really been struggling with [the politics of publication] lately because I think I have been more interested in getting [my work] published and out there in the research journals and have not worried if a lot of stuff went unsaid. But now I'm starting to go back and say, "I need to be more overt about my values; I need

to struggle to get that in [print]." But that's very difficult. It's very hard to get past an editor with some of that stuff.

All faculty members interviewed reported being torn, at some time or other, between the desire to change the writing and research of their disciplines and the need to produce conventional work to publish in established journals. Since the majority of the faculty I interviewed aimed to reach broader audiences (see chapter 4) as well as to cross disciplinary boundaries with their research (see chapter 5), the politics of publication became, at times, an issue critical to the pursuit of their scholarship.

Graduate and undergraduate students rarely engaged in the process and politics of publication, but their sense of ownership was still at stake when they handed in assignments, listened to feedback, and received grades from their instructors. The students I interviewed reported that their instructors allowed them to express their points of view in writing provided they argued for and substantiated their claims. Few students had encountered instructors who insisted on major revisions or changes in their writing. When they did, they had to make decisions similar to faculty members negotiating with editors: whether and how much to change the nature of the arguments or opinions expressed in their writing. Complying with major changes often meant securing a grade but not expressing one's opinion; resisting such changes meant risking a grade but expressing one's view. Students, particularly at the undergraduate level, reported modifying their claims to fit what they perceived to be the professor's agenda. One undergraduate student in nursing described how she changed her argument to accommodate an instructor: "I had an instructor, and we had dissimilar beliefs. I'd turn in a rough draft because I knew this. It was a good thing. She just ripped it to shreds. I thought my way was correct, and she thought hers was correct. Well, I revised it so it was what she wanted, but I didn't think it was very good. I got the grade, but it lacked my point of view." This student delivered what was demanded, a safe choice given that she was graded on the assignment, but she felt compromised in the ownership of her text, not unlike the psychology professor who reduced her opinion (and much of her data) to a footnote.

Occasionally students were willing to challenge instructors' views and defend their claims, even if it meant risking a grade. The students willing to assume such risks were either advanced graduate students completing their degrees or returning students—two groups who were either moving toward or had had professional experiences.

> I'm not afraid of disagreeing with a professor. If I present myself and my ideas and defend them in an appropriate manner, I'm not afraid of that. But if professors begin to tell me what I have to say, then it's their [writing], not mine anymore. And being the person I am, I would probably not conform to what they wanted me to do, and therefore, I would win for myself and lose in the course. (A graduate student in anthropology)

> I've gotten to the point where I'm willing to make a commitment on paper. I've said it in the best way that I know and presumably presented the best research available given whatever constraints. If [the instructors] don't like it, that's their prerogative. It's good and I know it. Now you may not agree with that, but I think it's good. (A graduate student in history)

These two students, both willing to assert their views and confront their instructors, were exceptional cases. More typically students, much like the faculty, were willing to negotiate the final revisions of their writing.

## Authority, Self-representation, and Narrative Strategies

So far, I have discussed *what* women said about establishing their authority in relation to their rank, their writing experiences, and the politics of publication. Furthermore, I have noted some reasons why women are more likely than men to encounter challenges to their authority: occupying marginal positions in institutions of higher education and society at large, not being perceived as authorities, and engaging in scholarship that challenges traditional disciplinary perspectives. Now I turn to *how* women talked about their sense of authority, how they narrated stories about their writing and research—their intellectual lives—to make sense of those experiences. While writers' narrations of their writing experiences are invisible—in fact, immaterial—on the written page, these narrations contribute, in very material ways, to the success or failure of scholars' work. The act of telling a story reveals how writers make sense of their writing and publication experiences, how they interpret their past experiences to anticipate future events. The stories that emerged during the interviews demonstrate the importance of narrative strategies in shaping a woman's sense of authority, her level of confidence, and her motivations for doing academic work. Because speaking and writing from a marginalized position can problematize a woman's sense of authority, the process of narrating and evaluating past experiences can become an important tool for how a woman meets challenges to her authority.

One narrative strategy common to women's stories was a move to establish distance from their writing. This strategy involved detachment from or even denial of textual ownership, a strategy that may be a direct consequence of the frequent challenges women encounter to their authority. Research on writer's block (Cayton), academic publishing (Spender, "The Gatekeepers"; Simeone), and graduate students' writing (Sullivan, "Feminism"), for example, suggests that women are likely to find academic audiences inhibiting because they represent traditional "gatekeepers" to the academic community, they determine what constitutes excellence in scholarship, and they have the power to pass judgment on as well as reject scholarly work. Creating a distance from one's text—denying ownership—is one mechanism for coping with inhibiting audiences. Peter Elbow notes that audiences can be a powerful field of force for writers, either enabling or inhibiting writing (see also chapter 4). Interestingly, while Elbow does not discuss gender as a factor in writer-audience dynamics, he does provide the example of a woman who could not begin to write until she had blocked out all audience considerations—that is, until she had created a complete distance between herself and the intended audience: "I ended up *without* putting a word on paper until I decided to hell with ———; I'm going to write to who I damn well want to; otherwise I can hardly write at all" ("Closing My Eyes" 51; emphasis added). Examples from four different faculty interviews illustrate some of the ways women established distance from their writing: by denying ownership of the text, by describing themselves as outsiders or "participant observers" in the academic culture, by reinterpreting discouraging writing experiences as positive learning experiences, and by describing writing and research as two distinct and unrelated activities.

An associate professor of psychology explained her writing process this way:

> I play a denial game, that somehow these pages that appear in a journal don't have a lot of connection with me. People who read them may or may not know who I am; it's just a paper. That's not logical, but those feelings do influence how easy it is to write it or not. I go through some weird disassociation between me and what I write. I'm almost willing to say anything and then see what kind of feedback I get from reviewers, to see if I can get away with it or not.

The denial game described by this professor works as a way of creating distance from her texts, of keeping critics at bay and challenging reviewers. If the written page has little to do with the author, it is easier for the author to make bold statements, to test new ideas, to assert her authority, to let the work be reviewed—in short, to succeed with writing and publishing.

A full professor in history used another strategy to distance herself from her writing; as a woman in a fairly male-dominated field, she situated herself purposely as an outsider:

> It's very much a male world. You're writing as a biocultural person; you are a female writing to the other culture. My academic life has been spent in the other culture. That's my record. But I have an extremely strong sense of myself as a woman, and I think it's different from being a man. I think it's not only different in a profoundly personal way, but it's different as a whole culture.

This professor described herself numerous times as a participant-observer during her interview, as a "stranger in a strange land." She used the participant-observer metaphor deliberately to achieve distance from her interactions with publishers, editors, and colleagues—people in positions to evaluate her work. By recognizing her position as an outsider and by purposefully positioning herself as such, she could more easily explain and meet challenges to her authority.

Reinterpreting past writing experiences was another strategy several faculty members reported using to achieve distance from their writing. An assistant professor of psychology described a serious obstacle she faced when writing her dissertation: her adviser read and criticized her dissertation in a painstakingly slow and critical manner—a page a day for a whole academic year—thereby delaying her graduation for over a year and seriously challenging her authority as a writer and researcher. Yet several years later, she reinterpreted this writing experience as a positive (though trying) learning opportunity, one she believed helped her become a critical thinker and careful researcher. Having succeeded with her dissertation—and having established her authority—against all odds, this woman now felt ready to face any academic challenge. In the following excerpt, she recalled both the difficulties and the learning opportunities this writing experience provided her:

> [My adviser] started going through the dissertation one page a day. I gave him a computer printout, and on every single page he wrote things like, "Where did this come from? I don't see any evidence for that. Why don't you read this article? How do you fit your ideas with these ideas?" I read this and was horrified. I went to him and said, "Could you please speed this up because I don't want to be here forever." And he said, "No, it takes a lot of thinking to do this, and I can't speed it up." In the end I decided to rewrite it the way he suggested. It took a long time. I went through the comments one by one because they were very precise and very reasonable. I recognized [the comments] as quality work and redid [the dissertation]. I really attribute a lot of my strengths to that experience, that intensive experience of having to go over every last word.

This writer's description of completing her dissertation illustrates how memories can be reevaluated, how experiences can be reinterpreted through the lens of time. The writer began her narration by stating that she was "horrified" by her adviser's response and ended it by stating that the response was "reasonable." Having survived the most serious challenge to her authority, she could now look back and reinterpret her past writing experiences. A later comment about her dissertation illustrates even more clearly this professor's process of reinterpretation. This excerpt begins with two contradictory statements that the writer then tries to reconcile through narration:

I thought it was really very *helpful*. It almost *destroyed me* personally. It's *devastating* to get a whole dissertation with [critical comments]. But it was *very instructive*, and so it was in my interest to deal with it. You just have to say, "I respect this; this is what I'm here for." It was very hard rewriting it. I think it was one of the hardest things I've ever had to do. I've forgotten a lot of that now, but that whole year just felt like a nightmare because on every page there were more difficult questions. . . . [But] it didn't inhibit my writing except that now I try to think about what I'm saying before I write.

This willingness to reinterpret and reevaluate difficult writing experiences in a positive light was common among the faculty members I interviewed. In retrospect, even the most negative and discouraging experiences with editors, reviewers, and advisers were reinterpreted as positive learning experiences. For the women I interviewed, then, an important part of learning to establish their authority as scholars was their ability to reevaluate and reinterpret negative writing experiences in a positive light.

Of course, negative writing experiences can discourage any writer —regardless of gender—and many writers find that dissertations are among the most difficult and demanding tasks they have ever faced. Gender, however, can complicate these difficulties because academic women are already positioned as "outsiders in the sacred grove" (as Aisenberg and Harrington note in the subtitle of their book) and may interpret negative writing experiences as direct challenges to their place and authority in the academy. Not all women will have the confidence to continue working under conditions as difficult as the dissertation-writing process described by the psychology professor; not all women have the confidence to reinterpret negative writing experiences as positive learning opportunities—rather than as personal failures (e.g., Cayton; Sullivan, "Feminism").

Yet another strategy of achieving distance from one's writing was described by an assistant professor of anthropology. She established her authority by defining research and writing as two distinct, separate activities. This professor evaluated her ability as a writer more negatively than any other faculty member in this study, but in contrast, she assessed her ability as a researcher very positively. I quote extensively from this woman's interview to illustrate the conflicts revealed in her narrative and the gender issues implicit in it. This professor, whom I will call Professor Smith from here on, presented this self-assessment of her writing ability:

> I don't enjoy writing. I'm not a writer. I don't enjoy the turn of the phrase. My husband is a writer, and he's very very good, and it's like he can't stand my writing. I'm just pretty straight forward, do what has to be done, I'm grammatically accurate. . . . I'm not a stylist or careful writer. So I don't write more than I have to. I'm quite productive—I mean, I just force myself to do it. I'm very disciplined, so if I have to write, I write. I have no illusions that I'm any good as a writer, so it makes it easier for me in some ways to just sit down and do it, because I know nothing very stylistic and wonderful is going to come out.

In contrast to her negative self-assessment as a writer, Professor Smith described herself as a successful researcher:

> I'm a very thorough researcher. I just stand on my work, my data. I think that's the strongest authority I can come from within a particular piece. I've been published a lot. I never had any trouble getting published. I always do [research] that no one is working on, and so I think people always want to publish my work because it's new. I'm always pushing ahead in what I'm doing. Both of the books I published are the first books in the field on these particular topics.

Professor Smith established her authority by defining writing and research as two completely separate enterprises; she denied her authority as writer but affirmed it as researcher. Like the psychology professor who described herself as playing a "denial game," Professor Smith kept potential critics, reviewers, and editors at bay. Her attitude enabled her to keep a distance from her writing, to welcome feedback, and to accept criticism: "I'm very non-ego-invested in my writing. In fact, I like people to be really critical because I don't feel [my writing] is very good. Criticism always improves what I'm doing."

A close look at the language Professor Smith used to describe her writing shows how institutional values placed on different types of discourse are deeply imbedded in her everyday language. In the following excerpt, Professor Smith described the types of writing she has done, implying a hierarchy of discourse types ("levels"):

> The book I'm writing now is for caregivers, so it's really very much for a lay audience. I also can write fairly technical [articles]; the paper I just wrote was technical. So I write at different *levels*. I'm not a *deep theoretician*, and I don't like semiotics and things like that, so I don't write at that *level*. I mean I write *one level below* or popular lay material.

Professor Smith's description of her writing reflects institutional—and some would say masculine—values, two sets of values that are closely linked, as scholars studying academic discourse and institutional histories have begun to notice (e.g., Bleich argues that academic forms of discourse reflect a genre/gender hierarchy; see chapter 1). Furthermore, Professor Smith's language also reflects a gender-based division of labor, as becomes clear when she compares her work with that of her husband:

> I can't really be a *heavy-duty academic*. It's not my style and I know that very clearly because I know that's how my husband is, and I'm not like that. We've got that role really well worked out, so I don't try to emulate him. That's what he does, that *real hard theory* stuff, and I don't do it.

Professor Smith's description of the work she does in contrast to her husband's reflects an institutional and gender-based division of intellectual labor: "hard theory" is still a predominantly masculine domain of scholarship and remains one of the most valued—and highest paid—forms of academic knowledge-making today (e.g., Simeone).

Professor Smith's presentation of herself as writer and researcher invites a feminist reading: one that would point out that women have been taught to be humble, not boastful; to credit others, not themselves; to play a subordinate role (to their spouse and to men in general), not dominate—in short, to be submissive and deferential. But Professor Smith's story can also be read as a success story, a reading I prefer. Her strategies of distancing herself from her writing have helped her to become a prolific writer and to establish a long and successful publishing history. She is a successful professional precisely because of what she has written; she has clearly joined the scholarly conversation of her discipline and has established herself as a valued and important member in her field. In fact, all women interviewed for this study were prolific writers and respected members of their disciplines; their ways of dealing with issues of authority were innovative and successful.

While Professor Smith's case is unique in many ways, it may also be representative of the strategies some women have to use, or feel they have to use, to establish their place—their voice and their authority—in academic discourse. Professor Smith's description of her work suggests that even writers with long, successful publishing histories will evaluate themselves according to institutional definitions of writing and research. Although Professor Smith has written two successful books (both groundbreaking works in her speciality), has published numerous articles, has given several talks (including a keynote address at the time of the interview), and has even written a best-selling restaurant guide during her years as a graduate student, she does not credit herself with the ability to write. The strategies of denial and distance, which faculty members like Professor Smith describe, remind us that a place for women in the academy is neither secure nor to be taken for granted.

# Portrait of a Writer:
# Professor Caraway
## "I need to be more overt about my values."

Professor Caraway, an associate professor of nursing, specializes in community health nursing, and at the time of this interview, she had just received tenure. She has won a number of grants and awards during her career and over the years has developed an interest in feminist approaches to research.

ONE OF THE HIGH POINTS WAS CERTAINLY TO GET THE PH.D. I got that relatively late in my professional career, I mean compared with where a lot of people get a Ph.D. in other disciplines. In nursing that's not unusual, but I've been professionally active since 1968, so it was almost twenty years coming. It was enormously exciting to get tenure, to be promoted to associate professor, also to be elected to the American Academy of Nursing last year. So there've been a lot of very recent high points. I got a first award, which is from the National Center for Nursing Research, so now I have federal funding, which has been a real exciting thing. Then I've been able to teach both a course in family violence, which is my area of research, and a doctoral course in feminist research methods, which was really fun. To be able to teach what you're really excited about is a high point. I love to teach, and I can teach a lot of different things, but to teach what you're really involved with, the research and the writing that's a part of your scholarly activities, is very exciting. All of this happened within the last five years.

One of the things I really like about this university is that the college of nursing is very strong as one of the units in the university. In a lot of institutions of higher education, the school of nursing is under the school of medicine—either literally or figuratively. Either the structure is such that the school of nursing is under medicine or the school of nursing is dominated by it. That's not true here, and that's one of the things I really like.

There is an underlying gender issue here. Certainly in nursing one would have to be enormously defensive not to feel gender issues, especially in today's world where gender issues are at the forefront. Nursing has a humongous gender issue with medicine, that traditional power structure has gone along gender lines. It's probably a real classic kind of thing. And in academia, there are also gender issues around the prestigious units in the university. They are generally male-dominated. And the less prestigious units— like social work, like education, like nursing—are more female-dominated. So you definitely feel that. That's one of the reasons that I have chosen to be at this university, to be in a place where the college of nursing has a kind of autonomy that I really enjoy. In my profession, I've also chosen to be, partly consciously, partly unconsciously, in community health nursing where there's a lot of autonomy.

I have had many mentors, and that's been very helpful. There has not been one person who has closely worked with me throughout, but there have been several. I think for a lot of people that works relatively well, because people don't stay in one place anymore. Even if you are the mentor—the kind of relationship where you totally guide one person all the way through—that takes a lot of energy from the mentor's standpoint. So there hasn't been any one person, but there have been at least, I would say, five or six different people [who] have served in that kind of role for me.

I've been encouraged to write since I was in high school. People have been giving me the message that I write well for a long time. But there were periods of time—when I went back for my master's degree—when I did very [poorly]. I flunked a paper; that did all kinds of terrible things to my writing ego. It was memorable because I had never expected to flunk a paper. I also suspect that being a woman, there's a tendency to equate what you write with yourself. So that if someone critiques it very harshly, I would suspect a woman would take that on more. Now that may not be true;

it may be that men are just better at hiding it. But I think a woman is more likely to think, "That reviewer doesn't like what I wrote; therefore, I must not write well."

I write quite a few memos, I do a lot of letters, a lot of articles plus presentations, speeches that are a little bit different from the articles, and lots of research proposals. I wrote one book and have been involved in a lot of book chapters, and I'm now getting ready to edit two other books. I must explain, I'm on a reduced teaching load this semester because I won an award. So that is freeing me up to do all this writing. You got me in a good semester—a writing fool.

I enjoy writing once I get into it, but the beginning parts are always hard. Getting going on a project when it's 70 percent done is a lot easier than it was in the beginning. I basically enjoy writing. I mean it's definitely work—it's not as much fun as going canoeing or things like that—but I do feel a sense of accomplishment, and I like to see something take shape. I don't like [writing] the research article any more or less than I like [writing] a chapter, and I don't like writing a speech any more or less. It's just a different mode, a different gear.

Memos and letters I stick in at odd little times of the day, and oftentimes I will clean up my daily writing at night, after the rest of the world has gone [to bed]. Writing an article, I try to do that at home. I have a personal computer at home. I have a study area that I work in, and I have books and piles of papers everywhere. Clutter does not bother me, as you can tell, although I get frustrated when I can't find things. I don't have to have everything cleaned up. I know some people like to have everything all cleaned up before they start to write. I will just get up and get books and stuff that I need as I'm going along. I go straight to the word processor and will write for a while, and then I'll often go back and rewrite the paragraphs as I'm going along. So the word processor is very helpful.

Rewriting is probably the hardest. Like when I get feedback from somebody, like when you send in an article, and the reviewers say, "Resubmit. Fix this and resubmit." Who are they to say there's anything wrong with it? I did it beautifully the first time. So why do they want to change it? You go through this thing, saying, "I like this sentence just the way it is. What do you mean it's awkward?" Sometimes you can see it, and other times it's just this ego thing, that you liked it the way it was.

The negotiating process with an editor can be enormously difficult and demoralizing. I had one article where the editor and I spent hours on the phone arguing, discussing whether certain phrases should be in there. That is an issue, but it's part of writing for publication. It comes with the territory. One has to accept that there is a lot of ownership that you give up. You take a certain amount of risk. I mean you sign a form when you send the thing in that says it's theirs, and so you sign over a lot of your rights. But for the most part, I think that the editorial process is helpful.

One of the things we've done here at the college of nursing—we haven't been too active this semester but the last couple of years—we have formed a writers' group. We submit manuscripts to each other and we read each other's stuff and give each other feedback. That gives you a sense that at least somebody else has seen it and didn't think it was a bunch of baloney, because it can be really scary to just send it off somewhere. All you know is that it's your baby, and you've worked really hard on it, but you don't know if it's worth diddly-squat. We try and give each other a lot of support on getting it out, on picking what journal we think would fit the best. That's really useful; it's very nice. I also have a good friend here at the college; she writes very well, and we read each other's manuscripts. So you have somebody who says, "Yeah, send it." It helps a lot to have people that you trust not to be ugly in their criticism.

The big thing that I've been struggling with lately, in my publishing, is trying to work out of a feminist framework. Does one publish in a journal that is specifically a feminist kind of journal, where you know that both your reviewers and your audience will be supportive and interested in that kind of viewpoint? Or do you publish in other kinds of journals, knowing, first of all, it may not get past the editors, but even if it does, that the editors will want you to cut that stuff out? They will say, "It's political and it doesn't belong in a research journal." You think that the readers of that journal might even be interested if they ever got a chance to see it, that they would be supportive and all that kind of thing. But do you preach to the converted or do you try to convince a whole new ball game? And frankly, I have not risked that in any big way. I mean I have not tried to get a feminist article published in a real established research journal. I've played my cards so that I have a variety of places where I've published. So I don't totally risk that—probably something I need to take on.

I would like to have more of my politics and more of my personal views come across than what a lot of people will allow. Some journals will allow more than others. In a sense, you have to leave part of yourself behind or you delete some of yourself out of it. Some of it has to do with the decision about where you're going to publish, whether you choose a journal that will take more of you in there or not. I have really been struggling with this lately because I think I have been more interested in getting [my work] published in the research journals and have not worried if a lot of stuff went unsaid. But now I'm starting to go back and say, "I need to be more overt about my values. I need to struggle to get that in." But that's very difficult. It's very hard to get past an editor with some of that stuff. I go back and forth. One day I say, "I'm only going to publish for people that I know will let me publish the way I want to," and then the next day I say, "It really needs to be in such and such a journal. I'm going to try there." It's an ongoing process. There's not a solid answer.

I see myself as having three primary audiences—that would be students, other academicians, and other nurses who are practicing out there. But I also sometimes write for other people working with battered women in whatever capacity, whether they are shelter workers or psychologists. I would like to be able to reach a wider audience. Women in general is an audience that I'd like to be able to reach in some way. I don't know exactly how to do that. I mean I haven't really worked very hard at that, but it's something I do believe in. As feminist researchers, that's one of the things that we do that's somewhat different from other research traditions: we do believe in trying to write for the general public of women. When I talk about women in general, I talk about women that could experience violence. It could have been in the past, or it could be in the future. So that's the audience I'm talking about. Battered women are women who are experiencing violence at this particular point in time. Any one of us could be battered at any time; last month we could have been battered and this month we're not being battered. One of the messages that I would like to get across is that being abused at one particular point in time doesn't make you a battered woman for life.

So you'll find a lot of feminist research in popular books in the bookstore. Sometimes the researchers will be criticized because

their work is not scholarly enough, and they are purposefully re-
leasing it. Of course, the question is, which do you do first? Do you
do the academic scholarly publications first and then the general-
public ones, or vice versa? Part of it depends on where you are on
the tenure track. There are practical considerations. Also, I have
funding from the federal government, and part of that funding says
that you will publish in scholarly journals, so you have an obligation
to do that. There just aren't enough hours in the day to write all that
needs to be written. I've done mostly academic kinds of writing so
far. But I did just publish an article in a nursing journal [that] is
almost purely a journal for practicing nurses. A lot of nurses read
that journal, so that was a different level of writing for me, and I
thought that was an important thing to do. It's tough to do all that,
to make it really meaningful at several different levels. You get
trained in the academic kind of writing; you have to change it some.

For the popular audience, you need to be more personal; there
needs to be more of you as a person. My general impression is
that the public is less interested in statistics and grouping people
together and more interested in individual stories and individual
voices. I think there's also a tendency, at least for publishers of
women's magazines, to want to sensationalize a little bit. In this
article I just did for a popular nursing magazine, they changed the
title. The topic was marital rape and women's health, and they really
sensationalized the title. That would have never occurred to me.
And yet you have to say, "Well, they know their readership, and
they know what will get people to read." I know that this is a topic
that a lot of times professionals don't want to hear about because it's
grim, and they oftentimes won't read that. So maybe you have to be
catchy and pull people in at some other level than purely appealing
to their scholarly interest. I feel ambivalent about that; its easy to
sensationalize this kind of work.

A lot of what we write—those of us who are in what [are] called
practice disciplines, like psychology (at least clinical psychology),
social work, nursing, medicine—we write both for academic (purely
academic types) and for practice-oriented audiences. Most people
in those professions are at least partly practice-oriented. If they
don't actually practice themselves, they have at some time in the
past, or they will at some time in the future, or they keep abreast of
what's happening in the practice field. That's one of the things—

that's my bias—that keeps the practice disciplines more closely in touch with the people they are studying or do research with: they do have that practice orientation.

For nursing, the combination of having a practice interest—an interest in the actual health of people and what your work does to impact that health—that combination of research and practice is very typical for nursing. The violence part of my work is atypical for nursing. There [are] not many of us in nursing doing work in this area, although it's growing. More people are getting into it, so it's not totally weird. In fact, I just came back from a conference on criminology. There were several papers on aspects of violence against women. So criminology is interesting to my work; sociology, especially sociology of the family, psychology, and medicine [are] starting to be interested in this area of research. My work is very much interdisciplinary.

I also work at the shelter for battered women so that I always have a sense, clinically, of what's happening. I have an immediate sense that what I learn has some value and some meaning on a clinical level. I both give and get back from that process. Also, to see what the women are doing and how strong they are and how well they do in spite of everything, that's the upside of this kind of work. It is really the best thing I do, as far as I am concerned, actually being there and working with the women.

# 4

# Expanding Communities: Writing for Academic and Nonacademic Audiences

THIS CHAPTER ADDRESSES ANOTHER QUESTION ASKED IN THIS study: how do women construct images of themselves and others—imagined and addressed audiences—in their writing? Theories of audience have moved into the foreground of composition studies in recent years because such theories focus attention on the social dimension of writing and raise important questions about the production and dissemination of written discourse. While the meanings of the term *audience* diverge into a number of different directions (see, for example, Park, "The Meanings of 'Audience'"), most scholars use it to indicate readers interpreting texts within social contexts that shape their expectations and contribute to the meanings of texts. Arthur Walzer, for example, points out that readers' expectations change according to rhetorical situations, that "the audience changes even if the readers do not" (155). By this he means that an audience of professional peers, for example, will play a different role when assembled at a national conference (expecting a well-timed, concise, and accessible talk), when reading a professional journal (expecting a well-developed argument that explains its methods, findings, and contribution to the professional literature), and when evaluating a grant proposal (expecting an argument for the significance of the work and the ability of the researchers to complete the work). I use the term *audience* here to invoke the social contexts that shape readers' expectations of texts and the term *reader* to refer to specific people writers described during interviews. Of course, the boundaries between readers, audiences, and writers are not always as clearly delineated as this definition suggests; Phelps reminds us that authors frequently become audiences and audiences become authors in the process of exchanging and revising work-in-progress (156–59).

Scholars in women's studies suggest that addressing audiences, particularly academic ones (which can function as "gatekeepers" to knowledge and power), takes confidence and authority, two qualities that are often challenged in women because of their historical exclusion from and marginal status within academic institutions. In her study of women and writing block, Cayton found that the women she studied, undergraduate students working on their senior theses, often had trouble imagining supportive and interested audiences: "They reported problems imagining an audience and meeting the sometimes conflicting needs of different audiences. Many doubted their ability to interest any real audience and expressed skepticism that the audiences they had in mind would respond favorably or appropriately to what they had to offer" (325). Furthermore, Cayton reports that the women she studied often felt they had disappointed an audience and apologized for having done so: "With surprising frequency, women also expressed a sense of having failed audiences, handing in notes of apology with rough drafts or chapter drafts of their projects" (327). The sense of having failed an audience was reported not only by students (the population Cayton studied), who are still learning how to contribute to ongoing discussions in their disciplines, but also by women faculty. Aisenberg and Harrington found that even senior faculty members tended to apologize for or diminish the importance of their work so as not to appear too bold, proud, or self-assured: "[A]pologizing [is] a mode of discourse many women adopt when they speak professionally. The prefatory disclaimer, for example, is common—'I just thought I'd mention,' 'I know it's a minor point but . . . .' Such remarks aim at self-effacement, the denial of self, at the very moment when the speaker is supposedly making a professional contribution" (69).

Women's tendency to apologize to their audiences for their work can be attributed to a number of reasons. First, women writing academic discourse are faced with living up to contradictory cultural norms: if they want to write with authority and conviction, they must engage in behavior traditionally coded as male (being assertive, even aggressive), and they consequently call into question their status as "real" women—at least as it is culturally coded (discussed in chapters 1 and 3). Simeone calls it a "no-win situation": "There is a restricted range of roles within which women can comfortably operate, yet they may be penalized even if their behavior falls within it. When women act in an "appropriate" fashion, they may be treated with chivalry and affection, yet their work may not be taken seriously. Yet, women who act in more stereotypically male ways may find themselves outsiders as well" (79).

Second, since women's concerns have often been dismissed, at least historically, as unimportant in the academy (and unworthy as topics of research), and since their talk—and writing—has been labeled trivial, illogical, or emotional (and sometimes still is), women cannot assume audiences will listen and take them seriously. Simeone notes that "women must prove themselves twice—first, their own authority and competence and then, the value of their work" (63). The fact that women in the past have published their work under pseudonyms (and successfully so) suggests that writers' gender—and other markers of cultural identity such as ethnicity and race—have played a role in the evaluation and publication of their work. Today the chances that texts will be evaluated according to their content, not the gender of the writer, have improved, and few women feel compelled to publish under pseudonyms. Yet the evaluation of writing is never an objective or value-neutral endeavor. Spender notes that there remains a "male dominance" among the gatekeepers of publishing who establish the criteria used to assess "scholarly excellence" and thereby determine "the 'fashionable' questions—and answers—which set the parameters in which individuals are encouraged to work, if they wish to be at the centre of the issues in their disciplines" ("The Gatekeepers" 187–88). Similarly, Brodkey notes that "authorship raises questions about authority that concern not only what writers have to go on, but also *what readers will accept* as worth their while to read and evaluate" (*Academic Writing* 27; emphasis added). Before women can begin writing, then, they have to imagine that their concerns matter; that their research is worthwhile; that audiences will take them seriously, show interest in their work, and evaluate their writing fairly.

Obviously, gender is not the only factor that affects writers' confidence and authority when addressing audiences. For example, studies of audience awareness show that experienced writers have developed more strategies for addressing diverse audiences than in experienced writers, and that they assess rhetorical situations more fully (e.g., Berkenkotter; Flower and Hayes; Kirsch, "Experienced Writers"; Rafoth). A large part of a writer's sense of audience, then, can be linked to such factors as years of professional experience and academic rank. In fact, most strategies for addressing audiences that faculty and students reported in this study reflect their level of experience, their academic training, and their disciplinary affiliations. Gender, however, is one factor that emphasizes issues of audience all writers must consider during composing.

## Academic Rank and Range of Audiences Addressed

Faculty members described a variety of audiences they addressed regularly, such as professional colleagues at national conferences and in academic journals, local peers at departmental meetings and in graduate seminars, as well as friends and spouses. Furthermore, they talked about audiences they wanted to reach, and in many cases, had been able to reach: general, nonacademic audiences who would be interested in or could benefit from their research, a finding I discuss in the last part of this chapter. In contrast, both undergraduate and graduate students addressed a very limited range of audiences; they named two audiences most often: professors teaching their courses and themselves. Generally, with more years of experience, writers had developed more ways of addressing diverse audiences, accommodating audiences with conflicting interests, representing themselves as disciplinary specialists, and responding to journal editors and peer reviewers.

As the debate surrounding invoked and addressed audiences suggests, there are important differences between the audiences writers invoke in their texts and the audiences they actually address with their writing (see Ede and Lunsford; Park, "The Meanings of 'Audience'"). Some scholars argue that the audience is always a fiction, by which they mean that writers can never fully know who will read their texts, under what conditions, and with what interests in mind (e.g., Ong; Long). They suggest that writers "fictionalize" audiences by invoking roles for readers within texts (through the use of conventions and appeals to readers' emotions, reason, ethics, and so on). Other scholars argue that while writers may never fully know their audience, they should still analyze and address "real" readers as much as possible because those readers can, at times, wield considerable power over writers (e.g., Mitchell and Taylor; Tomlinson). Invoked and addressed audiences represent two important dimensions of a writer's sense of audience. My own research on experienced writers suggests that invoked and addressed audiences interact in complex ways: experiences with past audiences affect writers' images of current audiences and lead to strategies for addressing future audiences ("Writing Up and Down" 47–50). Here I first report on readers that women in this study reported imagining during composing, and then I turn to the actual readers they sought out between drafts and encountered during publication.

Faculty

Faculty members described imagining a range of friendly and skeptical readers as they wrote drafts of their work. Imagined readers were usually based on experiences with actual readers, and writers evoked them selectively for specific purposes: to help them clarify their arguments, anticipate counterarguments, qualify claims, provide examples, sharpen the focus of their arguments, and address audiences with conflicting views.

> I imagine readers rushing madly through [articles] and relying heavily on abstracts to gather information. . . . The fact that there has to be an abstract means you must say things concisely, just a few words to get the essence across. (An assistant professor of psychology)

> When I'm writing at my best, I'm thinking of people I actually know in the field, because I know a lot of them. I know who's going to be reading this, and I know their writing. And I write to them and [to] graduate students that I've known here and other places. Then I put [the writing] through another filter of the most critical [readers]. It's good because [they are like] enemies that are really your friends, because they help you, they point out

weaknesses of your argument or [a] lack of organization. (A full professor of psychology)

When I did a survey of [doctoral] programs, I had to write it knowing the audience spanned people with opposite viewpoints, because it was such a political issue. So I tried to talk to both groups, to suggest alternative interpretations. (A full professor of psychology)

Faculty members imagined a variety of audiences reading their texts and used different rhetorical strategies to accommodate audiences with opposing points of view. Because all faculty members in this study were prolific writers and successful scholars, they had learned to be highly flexible with their choice of imagined audiences; they knew when to use and when to avoid the "focusing force" of an audience, as Elbow describes it: "An audience is a field of force. The closer we come—the more we think about these readers—the stronger the pull they exert on the contents of our minds. The practical question, then, is always whether a particular audience functions as a helpful field of force or one that confuses or inhibits us" ("Closing My Eyes" 51).

In short, faculty members interviewed for this study were successful writers who had mastered the discourse of their disciplines and had developed strategies for accommodating the various, sometimes contentious readers of their disciplines. However, when their writing was addressed to readers either in other disciplines or outside the academy—a goal *all* faculty members shared (discussed in more detail in the last part of this chapter)—they had to imagine new ways of addressing audiences with diverse backgrounds and different expectations. A full professor of history explained:

I bring this multidisciplinary approach, this macro-world approach [to my research]. There's always the problem of who is the audience. Audiences in the academic world are highly segmented. . . . I have worked myself out of an audience. The writing [problem for me] is how to reduce what I have learned into language that an educated person could understand regardless of special disciplines, special training, special orientation. That's difficult, very difficult.

Since the majority of faculty members were deeply committed to interdisciplinary work (discussed in chapter 5) and aimed to expand the communities of readers they reached, the problem of how to address audiences with diverse backgrounds and expectations became a critical one.

Once they had written drafts of their work, faculty members reported seeking feedback from friends, peers, colleagues, spouses, or writing groups before submitting it for publication. The kinds of feedback writers welcomed, the times at which they requested feedback, and the extent to which they made use of feedback all varied. By submitting drafts to friends and colleagues, faculty members established a sense of community that provided support, trust, and motivation to write. As Frey explains it, "A writer imagines who she is writing for and how they might respond. The motivation is intensely personal—to connect with someone else in a meaningful way. A nurturing relationship is important. Trust is important" (517). A nursing faculty member reported how a writing group to which she belonged functioned in just that way for her, providing valuable feedback and support:

> We have formed a writer's group [here at the college]. . . . We read each other's stuff and give each other feedback. . . . That's really useful; it's very nice. I also have a good friend here at the college; she writes very well, and we read each other's manuscripts. So you have somebody who says, "Yeah, send it." It helps a lot.

If faculty members did not belong to writing groups, then they had established working relations with a number of individual readers, such as colleagues, spouses, or friends with whom they shared work-in-progress:

> I don't share anything until I think I'm through with the first draft. Once I have written it, then I really like to get feedback. And my husband is one of my best critics. He just asked me some very basic questions that ended up really helping me. But I don't have to go back to him [often] because I have learned, in a way, to ask myself the major questions. (A full professor of psychology)

I do not let my work out at all until it's reached a certain level of perfection. Then there is a level of perfection that is achieved by having critics, friendly critics, read it and [make] friendly suggestions. And then there is the level where you have unfriendly critics who are reading it, who don't know you, and you don't know them, and they can make devastating comments. And if you are able to meet that level of demand in your work, then you have probably obtained a very high state of perfection. (A full professor of anthropology)

Besides consulting with individual readers or writing groups, faculty members also relied on national and international communities for feedback. A scholar in education and interdisciplinary rhetoric described the kind of feedback she sought for early drafts of her recently published book: "Since I was crossing all these different fields, I selected, for each chapter, one or two people who would give me good honest readings, who would not only examine the accuracy but would also raise questions. By then I had been working on the book for about four years, and I carved out this network of people across the world, and I just gave them the chapters."

When writers seek feedback from friends and colleagues, authority always rests with the writer, thereby making it easier to receive and accept criticism. Gere, describing the nature of self-sponsored writing groups—groups that meet on a voluntary basis—explains the role of authority in such settings:

In surrendering their writing, group members simultaneously give and accept authority. They give other individuals the right to express reactions and make suggestions and with that giving of authority goes the implicit willingness to credit (at least in part) the responses of their peers with authority. Because authority originates in individual members rather than in something or someone outside themselves, it always returns to them. They retain the right to leave the group, or to disregard the comments or advice of others. (50)

The fact that authority always returns to the writer when she chooses her first readers explains why faculty members were willing, even eager, to receive feedback, including tough criticism.

However, when the same kind of criticism comes from journal editors and reviewers, writers must surrender their authority, and they may lose the sense of trust and community that familiar readers provide.

Occasionally faculty members deliberately used the review and editorial process to receive feedback; one associate professor of psychology explained that she had come to rely on journal reviewers to learn about references she might have missed in the literature review: "I've used the review process to inform me about things that I've missed. A lot of reviews that I get back say something like, 'Well the discussion could be improved if she had read so-and-so's paper.' I feel comfortable enough with the process at this point that doing that is easier than doing all the legwork [reviewing the literature] and saving face to some extent." Obviously, using the review process in this manner requires confidence on the writer's part; she has to be sure enough of the quality of her work to anticipate suggestions for revision and not a flat-out rejection.

### Students

In contrast to faculty, both undergraduate and graduate students typically wrote for very limited audiences: professors teaching their courses and themselves. Excerpts from several students' interviews illustrate how dominant the professor audience was in students' writing experiences and how highly critical students imagined that audience to be:

I write for my professors most of the time; I write to people that already know what I'm trying to write. (A senior in psychology)

[I write for] professors. I address them very carefully. I assume that they know more than I do. So I write up [to them] to the extent that I can. (A graduate student in history)

My academic papers are for professors or for people who know already what I'm talking about. I try to figure out what the instructor wants, what I'm expected to do, what I have to put down in order to please an instructor—not necessarily please—but what they're looking for. (A senior in education)

I temper my writing as much as I can toward a particular professor's bent, but I don't think that's very easy to do. (A senior in history)

Most of the time, I would think that my readers are hostile. If it's a professor, I know they are hostile. (A senior in history)

I am concerned with saying things clearly. However, if the professor does not like what I say, I'll change it accordingly. (A senior in education)

Even advanced graduate students rarely considered writing for professional audiences in their disciplines. A graduate student in nursing said, "At this point [my writing] is mostly for professors. . . . To think about writing for publication is terrific; it's just not realistic."

As these students' comments illustrate, the classroom situation—students writing for a professor to receive grades—minimizes audience analysis for students, or at least it focuses their analysis on a single, powerful reader who reads with the primary purpose of evaluating writing and only with the secondary purpose of being informed or persuaded. Even when teachers deliberately ask students to write for other audiences, such as a group of peers or a general audience, students often do not develop much audience awareness. Park suggests that this difficulty stems from the fact that "the student . . . must somehow imagine or invent an audience in a situation where no audience naturally exists" ("Analyzing Audiences" 479). In other words, the teacher-audience is limited in scope and can encourage students to ignore the communicative purpose of writing.

However, despite the limited rhetorical situation of the classroom context, students in this study found ways to focus on other audiences, to write for themselves, and to define the writing tasks in their own terms. Some developed an interest in their topic and a commitment to their writing and decided that they themselves would become the primary audience:

I write for me based on what the expectations are, but not to please somebody's personality or way of thought. (A graduate student in nursing)

You should always write for yourself because it never works if you do anything in life for anyone else. . . . Please yourself first. (A graduate student in history)

[I write] pretty much [for] myself. When you're a student, you just don't really think about [readers] because you know that its going to be graded by a professor, so I don't pay much attention to that. Of course, you don't write sloppy and use poor English or anything like that, but I don't give much thought to [readers]. (An undergraduate student in history)

Writing can be boring, mainly a drag, until you get to that point when you really get invested in it, and then it becomes interesting. When you're really committed to it, then it becomes a wonderful search for information. (A graduate student in history).

In their study of student writers, Robert Brooke and John Hendricks found that the degree to which students create contexts that are meaningful for them while still fulfilling given assignments depends, in part, on how they see themselves situated within the classroom and the institutional environment. The researchers observed that students and teachers tended to negotiate their roles as readers and writers not only according to the writing task at hand but also according to the roles they chose to play in the larger social contexts of the classroom, university, and home community. Brooke and Hendricks explain:

[S]tudents and teacher will negotiate understandings of their classroom experience that support their sense of self, and these negotiations will influence their responses to the idea of audience. These negotiations involve issues of group membership. Classroom participants negotiate a sense of self largely by positioning themselves in relation to important social groups in the classroom and the surrounding institution. (53)

In Brooke and Hendricks' study, some students wanted to be included in the community of "successful writers" and therefore found ways to meet audience expectations and teacher demands, while others wanted to distance themselves from the community of writers and therefore would not address audience and teacher demands. Since all students interviewed for this study were above-average students, they usually found ways not only to meet teacher demands but to make the purpose of writing assignments their own.

## Addressing Nonacademic, General Audiences

Thus far I have discussed the range of *academic* audiences faculty and students address regularly, the strategies they have developed for addressing these audiences, the kinds of readers they imagine, and the feedback they receive. This description suggests that faculty members have developed successful strategies for addressing audiences and have gained the confidence it takes to succeed with publishing professional discourse, while students are still learning disciplinary conventions and ways of addressing academic audiences.

This description, however, is incomplete. *All* faculty members— and some students—also expressed the goal to expand their community of readers by writing for nonacademic, general audiences. Although the number of faculty members interviewed for this study is relatively small and the selection process was not random, the fact that all faculty interviewees reported either wanting to write or having written for nonacademic, general audiences is still striking. The kinds of audiences faculty members wanted to reach varied with the type of research in which they were engaged; usually it was a group of people who would be interested in or could benefit from the research they conducted. For example, an anthropologist studying home caregivers wanted to reach two audiences outside the academic community: caregivers and policymakers. Both groups, she recognized, would benefit from knowing more about the roles of caregivers within the family and the larger social structure. Excerpts from several faculty members' interviews illustrate the range of general, nonacademic audiences they hoped to reach:

> One of the things that has motivated me in my work as a historian is the hope that my work can have some little impact beyond the normal, narrow academic audience. . . . I don't want to take information and time from the people I interviewed and not feel

that [something] was going back into the population at large. (A full professor of history)

I want to become somebody who speaks to the public and who explains what it is that we do and what we know. I have a job to do; I have a mission; I have a destiny. And to achieve this destiny, I have to break the bonds of convention. My destiny is to learn how to be a writer in the real sense of the word and write for the public. (A full professor of anthropology)

I see myself as having three primary audiences—that would be students, other academicians, and other nurses who are practicing out there. But I also sometimes write for other people working with battered women . . . whether they are shelter workers or psychologists. I would like to be able to reach a wider audience. Women in general is an audience that I'd like to be able to reach [because] any of us could be battered at any time. (An associate professor of nursing)

I sat down to write a book that would be a comprehensive study that anybody could use, so it really speaks to the widest possible audience. (A full professor of education and interdisciplinary rhetoric)

I always want to talk to teachers. That's always my audience. I'm a teacher educator. I submitted an article for *Teacher*. It will probably not get me tenure, but it's a popular magazine that teachers will read. (An assistant professor of education)

I guess I should be writing for professors, but I'm not. What I always try, in my mind, I'm writing for the interested layperson in general. I think that good writing ought to be good writing for everybody. I absolutely hate to read historians who are just completely obtuse and are only writing for other historians. I write for the educated lay public. (A graduate student in history)

I try to address people that are nonprofessionals as well as professionals. So I write in a way wherein a person who doesn't know anything about the subject would be able to read and understand it. (A senior in nursing)

The goal to reach nonacademic, general audiences was universal among the faculty women I interviewed, and many reported having found ways to reach these audiences: for example, one woman had published in a popular nursing magazine, another in a pamphlet for the local community of health care specialists, and a third in a journal widely read by practicing teachers. Aisenberg and Harrington also observed that the women they studied (over sixty faculty members) often wanted to reach public, general audiences; they had a "sense of mission based upon belief in the educability of the general public" (78) and a desire "to be clear, understandable, to demystify the subject of experts" (77).

Whether or not the goal to write for general audiences is a gender-related phenomenon is a question that exceeds the scope of this study. On the one hand, it could be argued that because women tend to place a high value on relationships and on developing networks of communities (Belenky et al.; Gilligan), they would want to reach a wide variety of audiences. Brodkey observes, for instance, that "many academic feminists remain responsible to [at least] two communities: the academic community to which they have only recently been admitted and the community of women into which they are born" (*Academic Writing* 51). Many women I talked to fit that profile: they expressed a sense of obligation toward people they studied, and they valued their relationships with colleagues and friends. Furthermore, it is possible that because the disciplines represented in this study—anthropology, education, history, nursing, and psychology—typically involve the study of human subjects, in one form or another, and women tend to be attracted to—or channeled into—people-oriented fields (Aisenberg and Harrington; Bernard; Simeone), women's goal to reach broad, general audiences is particularly prominent in this study.

On the other hand, it could be argued that growth and professional development, not gender, account for the desire to reach nonacademic audiences: the longer a scholar works on a given topic, the more he or she may come to see its relevance to the general public. In fact, many academic scholars—both men and women—publish books addressed to public, general audiences once they have established their careers (see, for example, Thomas's reflection on biology, *The Lives of a Cell*; Tannen's account of gender differences in conversational styles, *You Just Don't Understand*; Allan Bloom's reflections on higher education in America, *The Closing of the American Mind*). The goal of reaching audiences beyond the academic one, then, is probably *not* unique to women. Other factors contributing to a desire to reach wider audiences could also include the ability to make money, to move into the public spotlight, or to display professional knowledge on a national scale. In short, the factors motivating an academic to write for general audiences could be wealth, fame, or power, in addition to the desire to share one's research.

However, the reasons women in this study provided for their goal of reaching nonacademic, public audiences—a "sense of mission" in their work, a desire to reach the populations they studied, and an obligation to make their research available to readers who might benefit from it—suggest to me that their goals were motivated by factors other than money, power, or fame. In fact, one woman reported earning no money for most of her publications:

> I never really published in a moneymaking place, and I think that may have to do with being a female writer, quite honestly. I was pressured to publish as quickly as I could, to take whatever I could. My first books, I got no monetary benefit from them. . . . And one of the books went into a third printing; it was used a lot. The third printing [came out] twelve years after it was first published, so it really had sold. But I never thought of money. (A full professor of anthropology)

Of course, interviewees are not likely to admit motivations that could be considered self-aggrandizing, but several faculty members I interviewed reported writing for nonacademic audiences despite the risk of receiving either no recognition or unfavorable reviews for such publications from tenure and promotion committees. A full professor of anthropology explained: "I try to make most of what I write at least usable to the community, as much as I can. I think we have to give back to the people we take information from, so I try to do that as much as I can. I don't get any brownie points academically for that, but it gives me the feeling that it's useful." Another woman, a nursing professor studying battered women, explained that her motivation for reaching the general population of women came from a desire to help victims of violence and to prevent other women from becoming victims. The goal to make research available and beneficial to the population being studied is a principle advocated by feminist scholars; and some faculty members, this nursing professor among them, consciously designed their research studies with feminist principles in mind.

Ultimately, however, the issue here is not whether women, more often than men, want to write for nonacademic, public audiences. Rather, the issue is how that goal interacts—or conflicts—with women's academic pursuits. As members who have only recently joined the academic community across different ranks and disciplines, women still have to be concerned about establishing their authority as scholars. Scholarship addressed to general audiences is often dismissed as naive or popular, and if such scholarship is produced by women, it can easily be interpreted as women's lack of seriousness or their inability to write academic discourse. As an assistant professor of history noted, "Historians typically don't sell books for public audiences. If you do, you risk professional delegitimization." Similarly, a full professor of anthropology observed: "[Writing for a public audiences] is given very low marks; there aren't any acceptable outlets for it. It's considered a second- or third-class activity. And yet it takes a great mind to translate the most important stuff into terms that other people can understand." In other words, writing done by academics that enjoys "popular" success is often denigrated within the academic community, regardless of the public recognition or monetary rewards such publications command. Brodkey suggests that "there is a sense, then, in which a text that is written by an academic for a designated academic readership and published by an academic press or journal might well be deemed an academic failure were it to succeed with a popular audience" (*Academic Writing* 25). Faculty members who choose to write for public audiences risk having their writing devalued within the academic community; they also risk their status as scholars, their reputation, and possible tenure and promotion. Women in particular risk reinforcing their roles as outsiders in the academy.

The women I interviewed were quite aware of having an obligation to publish in academic journals to establish their membership in the disciplinary community; to be evaluated as professionals by peers and committees reviewing their work; and, in the case of assistant professors, to achieve tenure. They reported that the conflict between their obligations to publish in academic journals and their desires to address public audiences created additional pressure and time commitments in their lives. Often they tried to negotiate this conflict by doing research relevant to *both* the general public and the academic community. Some women decided to wait until they had achieved tenure before publishing for general audiences; others wrote for general audiences before tenure but tried to publish with well-known university presses in order to "compensate" for the broad and sometimes practical appeal of their work.

> This book I wrote is very clearly for a broader audience. I felt I had to write the book; I just had to. So I did it. I don't know whether it's going to be rewarded, but it's being published by a pretty prestigious university press. I think I will probably get credit for it. The fact that John Hopkins is doing it makes a big difference. (An assistant professor of anthropology)

> In my book I'm going to make it just as clear as possible what I'm contributing to the profession of history. I'm going to make it as accessible [to a public audience] as possible given the constraint—the constraint being that I do, after all, have to get tenure. And I do have to get good reviews. (An assistant professor of history)

Although all faculty members in this study expressed a desire to reach nonacademic audiences of some kind, they did not necessarily dislike writing for academic audiences; rather, they hoped to *extend* their work to a range of readers who would not ordinarily have access to it. As an assistant professor of history put it, "I like academic writing, but I just know it not to be the whole job. . . . I can imagine continuing to do academic writing and doing other kinds." And a full professor of history explained:

> I realize I'm a professional historian, after all. In a professional journal you are addressing primarily other professional historians. And there are some interesting problems of interpretation that

one needs to investigate. But there is a part of me that still wants that other thing—the human story—to come through. . . . When I was a graduate student writing up this stuff I was absolutely determined that my first draft, at the very least, would tell the human story. There were sections [of my dissertation] I wrote in the first person because I wanted to convey the experience; I didn't want the historian to come between the reader and what had happened at one time.

Wanting to reach broader audiences, however, did not necessarily mean faculty members knew how to write for them; they reported that writing in new genres made new demands on their time and abilities. A full professor of anthropology reported struggling with writing for public audiences: "I don't know how to translate what I know into language that will capture the attention of people who are not members of my discipline." And an associate professor of nursing said: "You get trained in the academic kind of writing; you have to change it some [when you write for public audiences]." Even when faculty members had succeeded with writing for public audiences, they did not necessarily find the process satisfying. Articles can still be rejected, as one psychology professor had recently learned; they can be difficult to focus, as an anthropology professor noticed when trying to assess the knowledge nonacademic audiences could be expected to have; and they can be revised—even manipulated—by editors, as a nursing professor noticed when the title of her article was changed without her consent. She explained:

In this article I just did for a popular nursing magazine, they changed the title. The topic was marital rape and women's health, and they really sensationalized the title. That would have never occurred to me. And yet you have to say, "Well, they know their readership, and they know what will get people to read." I know that this is a topic that a lot of times professionals don't want to hear about because it's grim. . . . So maybe you have to be catchy and pull people in at some other level than purely appealing to their scholarly interest. I feel ambivalent about that; its easy to sensationalize this kind of work.

Like this nursing professor, scholars who have succeeded with publishing for general audiences have noticed the problems they can encounter with media representations of their work. For instance, Laurel Richardson, a sociologist, has described in a moving personal account the media's representations (and misrepresentations) of her work as she embarked on a book tour to promote her feminist research to a larger, public audience ("Sharing Research with Popular Audiences").

Women who pursue their desire to reach general audiences take a number of risks: they have to insist on the value of their scholarship within the academic community despite the tendencies of those communities to devalue popular publications; they have to commit more time to their writing if they are to meet both their academic obligations to publish in professional journals and their goals to reach nonacademic audiences; and they have to transform academic kinds of writing to be more accessible to general audiences. Because women already occupy a marginal position in the academic setting, writing unconventional forms of discourse for public audiences further challenges their authority. Aisenberg and Harrington assert that "the problem for women who reject the prevailing model for professional discourse is to find a countermodel that commands respect. How can women become insiders [in the university] and acquire an insider's voice of authority while questioning insider values? Where is the model for new forms of discourse?" (78). That, then, is the problem women scholars face when they desire to transform academic discourse and the audiences it reaches.

# Portrait of a Writer: Ms. King
## "I try not to use too many words, try not to jumble fifty-cent words."

Ms. King is an undergraduate in education and a first-generation college student. She reflects on the high and low points of her college education and describes writing experiences typical of many undergraduate students: completing assigned papers for classes, anticipating instructors' responses and criticisms, and writing under pressure against deadlines.

MY MOM AND DAD, THEY NEVER WENT TO COLLEGE. MY DAD started working when he was eighteen. He never got to go to college, but he really thinks people going to college and getting an education is just great. Even though I'm not doing this for him, when I do well, it really makes me happy to see that he appreciates it and is proud of it. I'm the oldest child in my family. I have aunts and uncles who went to college; one is a lawyer. I will be the third one in the entire family to go to college.

I've had some good experiences in college. I've really enjoyed it; it's been great for me. I've had fantastic professors for the most part, and I've been doing well. I learned a lot as far as my major goes. I find I very rarely have to do homework; I very rarely have to study that much. I thought I would be up all night, every night, studying and driving myself crazy. I thought I would have mean professors, but I don't. I've learned a lot, but it just doesn't seem as much like work as I thought it would be. It has been challenging, but I haven't been tearing my hair out or stressed out about anything. That's been the good part.

The college of education has a combined curriculum where, to study English, you take a certain English sequence. I'm taking the liberal arts sequence in English in addition to getting my teaching certificate, so that takes a little bit longer. You're left on your own a lot in terms of choosing your classes—almost too much. There's not much guidance. I always feel that advisers, they seem so inaccessible, so unapproachable, and they shouldn't be. Maybe they're not, but to me they seem very unapproachable. I haven't seen one in two years. I just send in my class registration forms, and I've always gotten all my classes.

Right now I have two history courses (neither requires any sort of writing; it's just tests) and two education courses (one of them does require a paper, and the other one requires an entire project to be written). I also have one English course I hate. I have a large paper due at the end of this semester, and I don't know what I'm going to do for it. I haven't even thought about it at all. I've taken all these English classes, and I still feel like I don't know anything. In this class we've got so much work and so much reading, and there are people in the class talking these big philosophical parts. I don't know what they're talking about, and I feel very inferior because I don't know what's going on. I know the end is in sight, but it's really getting to me, having to keep motivated. I've only got a few classes left. My grade point is really good; I just got to keep going.

I've had internships through the English department. For the first one, I put out a newsletter. I belong to an organization, and I am the editor of the newsletter, and so I used that for an internship. That was great because all I had to do was write everything down. There was no right answer to it. I just had to create ten pages of good stuff. I do that every other month; I switch off with another girl. I write the newsletter just for average folks, usually high-school-educated people.

I write papers and essays a lot. I've had instructors who have let me—let the whole class—be creative in their writing by not requiring a straight forward five-paragraph essay for everything. A little creativity makes it more interesting. That has been very helpful to me. I like writing academic papers; it's like an accomplishment, more or less. Once I get it done, it's like, "Wow, I know all this." So they have their good points. I like creative writing. I haven't done it in a while because I've been so busy with other things, but I do enjoy creative writing—short stories and things like that.

My academic papers are for professors or for people who know already what I'm talking about. I try to figure out what the instructor wants, what I'm expected to do, what I have put down in order to please an instructor—not necessarily please—but what they're looking for. I try to add some humor or lightness to academic papers just because, to me, reading straightforward pieces is the most boring thing in the world. If I know I can get away with some humor, I'll do it—if I know the instructor won't have a fit.

I'm more concerned with saying what I have to say clearly and concisely, keeping in mind it can't be some off-the-wall type of creation. But mostly I worry about getting it done. I try to be very—I don't know if *professional* is a good word—very formal, but without being stuffy. I try not to use too many words, try not to jumble fifty-cent words. I try to say what I have to say and get out. I don't try to be real fancy, because I think that's avoiding the issue.

I'm just very organized. I try to write a very organized paper and keep it within bounds of what I'm trying to say, making sure everything connects from the beginning to the end instead of going off on tangents. I think organization is probably my best part. I like the instructor to give a few guidelines, to an extent, because it helps me with organizing. I have this whole vast array of things I can do, and to have it narrowed is good. But when it's too narrow, I don't like that either because it may not fit my style. I like a little bit of structure; that helps very much.

I very rarely do drafts because I do it on the computer. I sit down and write it right there on the spot. And I usually turn in what I originally wrote. I pull my Lazyboy chair up to the computer, sit down in my blanket, and pull the keyboard down on my lap. That's where I do everything, right there. With the computer, I think I have more of a free flow because I can just type it. It takes less time to type than to write long hand, so I can get more out in less time. And if it's messy, I can just delete it. I don't have to scribble and recopy. I think it's much more organized that way. I am grateful that my father bought the computer; it's the best, an IBM.

Usually I don't do papers until the last possible minute because if I start thinking too early, they drive me crazy. So I usually start doing them two days before or the night before they're due. I write a rough outline, long hand, before I start. I write down what I want to say, how I'm going to say it, and how I am going to prove it. Then I try and get my evidence straight. I'll keep referring to my outline, reminding myself, "This is the track I have to keep on." I keep rereading what I outlined. I do all my revisions right there, everything. When I get to the end, I'll go through and read it one more time, making sure that's what I want [to say], and then I'll print it. Sometimes I'll do it in parts: the second night before [it's due], half of it, and the night before [it's due], the other half. I'm usually up till three o'clock in the morning. I always have the TV on; I'm drinking my Pepsi.

When I read somebody else's writing, I'm extremely critical. Everything from little grammar mistakes to conceptual mistakes just drive me crazy. When I type my boyfriend's papers—he doesn't have a typewriter—I just can't handle it. I have to keep in mind that I'm just typing, I'm not writing it, because I want to rewrite everything. That's the biggest thing. I want to restructure it totally, and I have to stop myself all the time from doing that. I do the same thing to my sisters' papers.

Academic writing that I don't know anything about is difficult when I feel insecure about the materials and have to formulate some way of saying what I have to say and I really don't know what I'm doing myself. I'm always afraid that the professor or instructor is going to get it and say, "You don't know what you're talking about." That's what I think a lot. If I don't know what I'm talking about, then I find it very hard to act like I do.

I feel uncomfortable when I really don't agree with an instructor. I will try to tone it down a little bit, what I'm writing, because it all comes down to the stupid grading system. It all comes down to A's or B's or whatever. Even though it seems so arbitrary, that's the only thing a person has to judge you [on]. And if I'm going to argue or hold a conflicting view with a professor who can't handle it and will say, "Well, D for you," then forget it. I will write whatever they want to hear just for the sake of the grade.

I had a paper due in the English class that I hate; I turned it in a few weeks ago. I had a very hard time with it because I felt very insecure about what I was writing. I really didn't know if I was right or not. That was very hard. How can I write this paper to convince somebody else when I don't know what I'm talking about? I haven't received it back yet. I want this paper back to find out if I was anywhere close. It's been three weeks and that makes me really angry.

As far as school work goes, the feedback I get is basically what the instructor writes down, the comments. I would hate talking to instructors; it usually makes me very nervous. I'd rather they wrote comments than my having to go up and discuss it. I just don't feel confident enough. There are times when I don't necessarily agree, but I have yet to argue about anything. But then most of my grades have been fine; I haven't really had to [argue about my grades]. There's only been one paper where I really disagreed. I just threw it in my bag and walked away. I was so mad, I didn't want to say anything to [the instructor]. Because if I would have approached her right at the time, I don't think I would have been too nice about it. It was the end of the semester, and I didn't care anymore.

I'm not as good a writer as I thought I was. When I was in high school, I could write circles around everybody. But coming into college, it's shifted. I was a yearbook editor in high school, and I wrote just about every piece of copy in our entire year book. But once I got into college, there were better writers.

# 5

# Crossing Disciplinary Boundaries: Transforming Academic Writing and Research

WOMEN ENTERING THE ACADEMY ARE NOT ONLY INTERESTED IN gaining access to the institutions that have historically barred their presence. They are also interested in transforming the disciplines in ways that are meaningful to them, in ways that include their interests, their presence, and their life experiences. Now that women are entering the academy in greater numbers and in more disciplines, they are reexamining every aspect of academic institutions: the language used to ask research questions, the kind of research questions deemed important, the kind of data included in—and excluded from—research studies, the conclusions drawn from research, and the type of writing used to convey findings and interpretations. In this process of reevaluating the disciplines, women are both challenging and changing—however slowly—the nature of the academy. What is at stake, then, is nothing less than "reconstructing the academy," as Minnich, O'Barr, and Rosenfeld suggest in the title of their book. They argue:

> Feminist scholarship is no longer simply a criticism of or compensation for old errors, nor is it an isolated specialty practiced only by a few. It can and should enter critically into all efforts not just to extend but also to redefine knowledge. Yet, in so doing, feminist scholarship does not become just one among many new voices. It retains its *commitment to critique all knowing*. Women

and women's studies are now included in the academy, and feminist scholarship is spreading throughout the curriculum. But we do not yet have a transformed academy, as we do not yet have a transformed world, in which all humans can be properly included. As we insist not only on being in, but also on being fully present as, ourselves, to and for each other, we set the terms for that transformation—and continue the quest to understand ourselves, others, and understanding. (6; emphasis added)

How fundamental and far-reaching the feminist critique of the academy is can be seen by examining the kinds of basic premises feminist scholars challenge. In chapter 3, I discussed how Jones reveals androcentric biases in definitions of authority and calls for new ways of conceptualizing what being an authority or having authority entails. Minnich and her colleagues offer a similar critique of definitions of "reason":

> The realization that notions of reason and of maleness have been conflated and that the consequent gendered reason has been placed at the center of definitions of what it means to be human not only clarifies one deep and dangerous way in which women were defined by and for men but also points us toward the *need to reinterpret reason*—and so, of course, education as well. Such revelations are keys to unlocking the door of the academy if we are to enter, and then to leave, whole. (2; emphasis added)

Transforming the academy, if perceived in the terms described by Minnich and colleagues, becomes a monumental task: it challenges all aspects of the academy, from examining the most basic premises upon which disciplines are based to defining new goals, methods, and ways of doing research within and across disciplines. For women to engage in such a fundamental critique of the academy (and their disciplines) means treading on thin ice: on the one hand, women are working to join the disciplines (and often still feel they must prove their ability to master traditional scholarship); one the other hand, they are questioning the very nature of the academic enterprise.

In the interviews I conducted, women—in particular, the faculty—described how they were engaged in changing and transforming the work of their disciplines, a process often begun long before feminist scholarship gave voice to such concerns. Although I did not set out to study women's goals for changing the nature of their disciplines (and the interview questions focused on writers' sense of audience and authority), the sheer number and diversity of comments on disciplinary change and transformation compelled me to report on this aspect of the interviews. In the previous chapter, I reported on some aspects of the transformative process, as expressed, for example, in women's goal to reach nonacademic, general audiences. Here I present the contexts of women's work and visions—women who are changing the research and writing of their disciplines in profound ways.

## Engaging in Nonmainstream and Interdisciplinary Work

The majority of faculty members interviewed in this study—fourteen out of fifteen women—described their work as situated outside the mainstream of their disciplines or as interdisciplinary in some respects. The features that placed their work outside the mainstream of their disciplines varied: some included the methodology used, the kind of research question asked, the perspective brought to the topic, and an interdisciplinary framework used to interpret data. In this chapter I discuss interdisciplinary work—work that transcends disciplinary boundaries and methodologies—and nonmainstream work—work that takes an unusual approach to disciplinary research (such as the use of ethnographic methodology to study history)—together, not because they resemble each other, but because both situate women's work at the margins of their disciplines and both can challenge women's authority as scholars and researchers. The distinction between interdisciplinary and nonmainstream work itself is not critical to the discussion that follows; I mention it here only to avoid giving the impression that there is great homogeneity among women's scholarship. Excerpts from several faculty members' interviews illustrate the ways in which they described their work as interdisciplinary or outside the mainstream of their disciplines:

> I have to read literary criticism, and I have to read philosophy. . . . I make use of anthropology to crack the contents of minds. (An assistant professor of history)

Criminology is interesting to my work; sociology, especially sociology of the family, psychology, and medicine [are] starting to be interested in this area of research. My work is very much interdisciplinary. (An associate professor of nursing)

My writing includes a lot of pulling together theory and empirical data from other fields and presenting them in a way that anthropologists can understand. (A full professor of anthropology)

When you are working on problems that have a connection to the real world, a lot of different processes interact that don't settle out in terms of academic disciplines. What you end up with are principles from social psychology, for example, that influence cognitive processing. Well, cognitive people don't pay a whole lot of attention to what's going on in social psychology and vice versa. . . . So I think you end up with a slightly different perspective on things . . . . Principles from social psychology, anthropology, sociology, and [even] political science are all relevant [to my work]. (An associate professor of psychology)

The violence part of my work is atypical for nursing. There're not many of us in nursing doing work in this area, although it's growing. More people are getting into it, so it's not totally weird. (An associate professor of nursing)

These quotes echo each other, although faculty members worked in different disciplines and studied vastly different topics. Not only were the majority of women I studied engaged in interdisciplinary or nonmainstream work, but the same was true for the women Aisenberg and Harrington studied. They observed that the "overall rate of non-mainstream scholarship was high—about 70 percent, with roughly half of the women . . . engaged in studies focusing on women and another fifth in unconventional studies of subjects other than women" (103).

It can be argued that interdisciplinary scholarship is, in many ways, a recent phenomenon, typical of academic work in the second half of the twentieth century. In fact many universities have set up interdisciplinary programs in recent decades, and *both* men and women have increased the amount of interdisciplinary work they do. In some circles of the academy, it is even highly fashionable to engage in interdisciplinary work, as is illustrated, for example, by the recent foray into legal discourse made by literary scholars like Stanley Fish. At issue here, however, is *not* whether there is a correlation between an increase in interdisciplinary work and women's scholarship. Rather, at issue is how women interpret their work, define their goals, and position their scholarship and themselves within their disciplines and the academy. The women I interviewed perceived their work to be at the margins of their disciplines, not at the center. That sense of marginality—whether real or imagined—adds another challenge to women's sense of authority, as several faculty observed:

When you're working in an interdisciplinary area such as I am trying to do, you have to become like a child in the other field. I may be an adult in anthropology, but I'm a child in the field of technology innovation. So I'm trying to learn that field and incorporate its theory with anthropological theory and reflect it back to experts in a way that seems authoritative. *It scares me. I'm constantly uncomfortable.* I have to read more and more sources. It leads to an overload [of reading] in order to establish authority in a new field. (A full professor of anthropology)

Interdisciplinary research is difficult because I'm constantly reading in a variety of fields. *I always worry* that I haven't done it thoroughly enough. (A full professor of education)

Furthermore, it can be argued that because academic scholars are trained throughout their graduate education to make "original" contributions to research, it is not surprising to hear women describe their work as unique, original, atypical, or nonmainstream. However, women interviewed in this study described their work not only as unconventional but also as challenging the research traditions of their disciplines, as crossing disciplinary boundaries, and as concerned with issues of interest and importance to women. Together these features do more than distinguish women's work as original, unconventional, or nonmainstream; they raise questions about women's disciplinary "home bases," about appropriate publi-

cation forums and conferences, and about the evaluation—and recognition—of their work.

Among the features Aisenberg and Harrington found typical of
women's scholarship were the "placing [of] subject matter in a cultural context" (90), "a fascination with subjects combining theory
and reality in a variety of ways" (94), the "transcending [of] disciplinary boundaries" (96), and a "preoccupation with seeking social
change" (98). Aisenberg and Harrington summarize the features of
women's scholarship this way:

> Overall, women scholars are heavily engaged in integrating knowl-
> edge. Their work *combines* disciplines, *combines* theory and re-
> ality, *combines* a commitment to change with a commitment to
> humane study. Its approach to knowledge is inclusive to the point
> of ambiguity, rather than exclusive to the point of certainty. Its
> social vision is of an integrated whole with the characteristics and
> interests of diverse groups honored and supported. (105; Aisen-
> berg and Harrington's emphasis)

In my study, faculty members who engaged in "work [that] combines disciplines" or "combines theory and reality" reported that
their work allowed them to ask a whole range of new research questions, as an associate professor of psychology explained:

> A lot of questions that I investigate come from my own experi-
> ence, my own observations of what happens in the real world,
> as opposed to being logical extensions of things that I read in
> journals. . . . I tend to think that some of my work is more cre-
> ative because of it. If you don't get tangled up in the esoteric
> arguments in the literature and do work that makes sense in
> terms of other people's concerns and what is important [in] your
> own experience, I think your work tends to be richer, more
> complex.

Similarly, Bateson, in her study of five prominent scholars' lives,
suggests that interdisciplinary work invites creativity and allows for
new visions of scholarly work: "It . . . seems probable that the most
creative thinking occurs at the meeting places of disciplines. At the
center of any tradition, it is easy to become blind to alternatives. At

the edges, where lines are blurred, it is easier to imagine that the world might be different" (73).

Since the women I interviewed tried to imagine a world that might be different—at least different to the extent of allowing them a voice and a place in it—they were apt to seek out work that allowed for alternative visions of knowledge and research. Interdisciplinary and nonmainstream scholarship, then, allows women to ask new research questions, to redefine the traditions of their disciplines, and to work on issues that are of interest and concern to them. At the same time, engaging in such scholarship carries a number of serious risks for scholars, and for women in particular.

Scholars who study unconventional or interdisciplinary subjects face a number of potential problems, such as keeping up with the publications of several disciplines; finding forums for publishing their work; justifying the importance of their work; receiving funding; and in the case of tenure decisions, finding reviewers who are competent enough to evaluate their work fairly. For women these potential problems can compound issues of authority and can highlight their already marginal status within the academy.

One of the challenges interdisciplinary scholars face is making serious time commitments; knowing more than one discipline can be an enormously challenging task, given the proliferation of subdisciplines within disciplines, the ever-narrowing specializations of scholars, and the growing number of professional journals and conferences. Engaging in interdisciplinary work not only entails keeping up on an extended reading list but also knowing the history, the jargon, the ways of reasoning, and the current debates of several disciplines—all of which takes years of immersion and participation in professional forums. Furthermore, scholars engaged in interdisciplinary or nonmainstream work must find forums for publishing their work, a task critical to tenure and promotion decisions, and ultimately, to their success—or failure—as scholars. A professor working in interdisciplinary rhetoric reflected on the difficulty of publishing interdisciplinary work and addressing audiences with diverse backgrounds:

There are journals that wouldn't even touch my stuff [because it's interdisciplinary]. And there are journals that would be open to my work, but they're not very prestigious. The problem is locating more prestigious journals. . . . When you talk about interdisciplinary matters . . . the audience is never as predictable as it is in traditional disciplinary writing. When the audience is composed of people from sociology, anthropology, and literary studies, whom do you write to? When you're doing work where you've got more than one audience, you have a greater burden to do an initial setting up of the argument. You're not banking on a preconceived set of assumptions; you have to define very carefully where you are.

In terms of evaluation, faculty members pursuing interdisciplinary work face the question of who will review their work within local and national academic communities. Reviewers are likely to be trained in only one of the disciplines relevant to interdisciplinary work and, therefore, are likely to evaluate interdisciplinary work according to standards limited to a single discipline. Tomlinson explores the dynamics of the review process conducted by readers with diverse disciplinary backgrounds: "[I]nfluenced by their various discourse communities—their disciplines, departments, and campus committees . . . readers essentially create the text as they read" (94); thus, they evaluate it according to their disciplinary training and biases. While it is true that all readers "create" the texts they read to some extent, scholars engaged in interdisciplinary work cannot rely on a core group of readers who—whether friendly or critical—at least share a set of basic assumptions and goals. A professor working in interdisciplinary rhetoric explained: "Just by virtue of being involved in interdisciplinary work, you're always crossing different disciplinary bases. . . . So much interdisciplinary work doesn't have a professional home."

In a similar vein, Cheryl Geisler has reflected on the "benefits and hazards of multi-modal research" (45) in her own work. She notes that using multiple research methods and addressing multiple academic communities has at least three "costs" associated with it: the time it takes to conduct such research, the effort it takes to make it comprehensible for several audiences, and the reception—and evaluation—it receives by scholars who may lack an interdisciplinary perspective (46–47). Like the faculty members in this study, Geisler concludes that for her the benefits outweigh the costs of multi-modal research, yet she remains acutely aware of the risks she faces as a yet untenured professor. The potential obstacles scholars face when engaging in interdisciplinary work, then, are numerous; they range from keeping up with new scholarship in several disciplines to finding a forum for publication and being evaluated by colleagues who may not have the interdisciplinary expertise necessary to evaluate work competently. Scholars whose work crosses disciplinary boundaries are often already at the margins of their home disciplines; women engaged in interdisciplinary scholarship are likely to highlight that marginality.

"Given the professional costs and moral dilemmas of pursuing nonconventional work, why do women persist in this effort?" (105), Aisenberg and Harrington ask. Their speculative answer includes three parts: (1) "established bounds do not admit the questions women want to ask and answer"; (2) women "want to gain understanding of a subject by immersing it in, rather than abstracting it from, the untidiness of human activity"; and (3) "out of their increasing consciousness of their own subordination, women are newly examining the allocations of power both in specific social institutions and in the larger society" (105). The faculty members interviewed in this study provided similar explanations for their motivations to engage in interdisciplinary or nonmainstream work—desires to interact with the people they studied, to make their research available and useful to general audiences, and to change institutions and society at large. A full professor of history explained the motivation for her work:

> I am fairly personally engaged in the history I write. It means a lot to me. People I write about mean a lot to me. The fact that I owe something to ordinary rural people who are willing to talk to me and share their memories with me—it's all very personal and very important. And when I write, I really write with those things in mind; that's who I owe something to. . . . Ultimately it's not the professional recognition that my work gets that matters.

This professor describes one of the goals that unites interdisciplinary scholars: the goal to make research meaningful to "ordinary" people. Brodkey describes other goals interdisciplinary scholars share: "Interdisciplinary communities share a picture of reality, and it is that vision of the way things are, and *the desire to change that reality*, that organizes language use around theories that would reconstruct the world, rather than around methods that merely reproduce it" (*Academic Writing* 36; emphasis added). This "desire to change reality," to "reconstruct rather than merely reproduce the world" inspired many of the faculty members I interviewed.

While interdisciplinary scholarship promises to change, not just reproduce, knowledge, it also has a number of limitations. Fish, for example, points out that interdisciplinary scholarship can amount to nothing more than redefining disciplinary boundaries: "The blurring of existing authoritative disciplinary lines and boundaries will only create new lines and new authorities; the interdisciplinary impulse finally does not liberate us from the narrow confines of academic ghettos to something more capacious; it merely redomiciles us in enclosures that do not advertise themselves as such" (18). Furthermore, Fish argues, true interdisciplinary scholarship remains an impossibility if its goal is to open up existing structures of knowledge in order to examine—and expose—their cultural and political mechanisms. That goal can never be achieved, Fish explains, because one can never stand outside one's cultural and political system: "Either, the vaunted 'blurring of genres' (Clifford Geertz's now famous phrase) means no more than that the property lines have been redrawn . . . or the genres have been blurred only in the sense of having been reconfigured by the addition of a new one, of an emerging field populated by still another kind of mandarin, the 'specialist in contextual relations'" (19). Fish's point about the limitations of interdisciplinary scholarship is an important one; it questions the very feasibility and possibility of interdisciplinary work. While it is true that one can never escape or stand outside one's cultural system of knowing, one can still make choices within that system. And the faculty members in this study reported that choosing to engage in interdisciplinary scholarship offered them viable possibilities for transforming the traditions of their disciplines.

## Visions of Transformation and Change

Women interviewed in this study, faculty members in particular, expressed a deep commitment to their work and to changing the nature of the academy. Heilbrun suggests that "women who are at the margin of the society and of the university no longer wish only to examine that marginality; rather, they profoundly desire to alter the nature of discourse that defines margins and centers" (35). In the following excerpts, women discussed the kinds of commitments they had made to their work:

> I have a tendency to get very committed to whatever I'm doing. I get very deeply involved. . . . I do it with a sense of integrity, a sense of doing it on its own merits, *for its own sake* rather than for anything you might call careerism. I've never been career-oriented. (A full professor of history)

> I just happened to get involved in something I cared so deeply about, it became a *life's work*. So for me that kind of work is a lot of fun, but it's not true for others. Nothing I do has a formula, which makes it more difficult but also more exciting. I really like doing new things that are different, sort of blazing new trails. (A full professor of education and interdisciplinary rhetoric)

> What shocks me is the discovery that there are people for whom history is a career rather than a *vocation*, who say, "Let's see; nobody has written about this. I can build a career out of this." What happens is that they write very mechanistic, super-impersonal history that almost manages to remove the original actors from the picture. That bothers me a great deal. . . . I hope that over time I don't lose what I think is that very important value: to portray real human beings and to portray real human predicaments. (A full professor of history)

Granted, a sense of commitment is common in the lives of *all* scholars, men and women, and many faculty members make serious sacrifices to pursue their intellectual interests. But what matters to the issue of gender here are the *kinds* of commitments women make and the *consequences* those commitments have in the academic world. For example, the commitment to do work "for its own sake" might entail loss of financial rewards and professional recognition; the commitment to "portray real human predicaments" goes against the grain of much traditional historical analysis (although debates continue about the degree to which the writing of history is and should be shaped by narrative elements, e.g., MacDonald, *Professional Academic Writing*); and the commitment to "write for the public" (discussed in chapter 4) adds additional work and time commitments to women's lives. Together these commitments pose serious risks to women's authority and to their success as scholars in the academy.

Furthermore, some women also wanted to change academic forms of discourse:

> Now that women are going into anthropology, I think there has to be a modification through the way women write and see things. . . . I think that as women go into this field . . . they'll begin to change the "good old-boy system" to a more holistic system. That is what I see, in the end—my purpose of doing this. Learn to do it their way, let them believe that I have credibility in the network, and then say what I have to say about possible improvement or addition to this particular methodology. (A graduate student in anthropology)

> It's the conversational mode that I would prefer to adopt as I'm writing. . . . I see myself as a cultivator of human relationships, and I imagine my world as one in which relations between individuals and conversations come first. I know that's something quite foreign to a good many male colleagues who think that those kinds of interpersonal relationships have no place in the work place. (An assistant professor of history)

As these comments suggest, some women in this study were interested in transforming the nature of academic discourse in important ways. The comment about wanting to write in a "conversational mode," for example, corroborates claims made by sociolinguists (e.g., Coates; Tannen), psychologists, and educators (e.g., Belenky et al.; Gilligan) that women prefer a cooperative, conversational style in speaking and writing over the competitive, antagonistic styles now prevailing in educational institutions and many other public forums. Frey, for example, has expressed an attitude similar to that of the history professor quoted above—wanting to avoid writing in the "adversary method":

Many of my feminist colleagues and I do not want to use the adversary method anymore, if we can get away with it. But this does not mean that all women or only women have trouble using [the adversary method]. In other words, it does not mean that it is "unnatural" for women to use the adversarial mode. Such a statement would misrepresent history in general and the histories of feminism and women's scholarship in particular, as well as the complex question of what it means to be a woman. (518–19)

Feminist scholars, then, are *not* arguing against writing and teaching argumentative forms of discourse; rather, they are calling for *expanding* the kinds of writing practiced and published in the academy (also discussed in chapter 1).

The changes in academic discourse that feminist scholars—and women in this study—advocate are taking hold in various forums across the disciplines. Feminist scholarship has been a powerful catalyst for change that is now sweeping across disciplinary and gender lines. Both men and women have begun to question and change academic scholarship and writing in recent years. "Brave experimenters" (520), as Frey calls scholars who are willing to write and publish unconventional discourse, are beginning to produce new forms of research and writing. In composition studies, for example, the publication of Mike Rose's *Lives on the Boundary* has spurred interest in autobiographical and intellectual histories. Autobiographical essays are now appearing alongside scholarly essays in edited book collections (e.g., Moran) and even in mainstream journals; the February 1992 issue of *College Composition and Communication* included several personal essays (McQuade; Sommers; Zawacki) as well as an essay written in multiple voices (Clark and Wiedenhaupt). As these examples illustrate, scholars from various corners of the academy and of both genders are challenging and changing the nature of academic discourse.

One of the changes advocated by the "brave experimenters" is for scholars to situate their research in the personal and historical settings in which they find themselves. Tompkins, for example, explains that we have been taught to avoid referring to personal experiences in our academic writing, a move that makes us believe our private lives are separate from—rather than a result of—the research and knowledge produced in the academy ("Me and My

Shadow" 169). Because using personal experiences as evidence is often dismissed as anecdotal, unreliable, and irrelevant, academic discourse tends to disguise its sources of authority. Bleich notes that "reference is rarely made to actual human experience even though it is assumed that *some* aspects of *someone's* lived experience renders the discourse rational to begin with" (18; Bleich's emphasis). And Elbow observes that by disguising sources of authority, academic discourse becomes exclusionary: "[A]cademic discourse also teaches a set of social and authority relations: to talk to each other as professionals in such a way as to exclude ordinary people" ("Reflections" 146). Like Tompkins, Bleich, and Elbow, some women interviewed in this study questioned the "disguised authority" of academic prose. A professor of nursing reflected on the problem of how to include her personal and political values in publications:

I would like to have more of my politics and more of my personal views come across than what a lot of people will allow. Some journals will allow more than others. In a sense, you have to leave part of yourself behind. . . . Some of it has to do with the decision about where you're going to publish, whether you choose a journal that will take more of you in there or not. . . . I go back and forth. One day I say, "I'm only going to publish for people that I know will let me publish the way I want to," and then the next day I say, "It really needs to be in such and such a journal. I'm going to try [to publish it] there." It's an ongoing process; there's not a solid answer.

Some faculty members speculated whether and to what extent gender was a factor in shaping their research and writing:

In talking to other women in my field, I come to find out that they worry about meaning in their work. Most of them are ambitious but feel the conflict between their ambition and doing something useful. . . . There is this struggle: "Do you buckle down and play the game [doing traditional work] or do you do what you want to, what you feel comfortable doing?" (An associate professor of psychology)

I am not ambitious in the sense in which I see men as ambitious. I'm a full professor now, and I feel I would rather produce something that enriches my life while I'm doing it, produce something that I am fully satisfied with, that I think is meaningful and not just an empty exercise done to please my peers or whoever is going to pass judgment on me. Unfortunately, the pressure to publish in academic life militates against those kinds of feelings of satisfaction. (A full professor of history)

Many women I interviewed in this study had begun to transform the academy—specifically, in ways of writing, conducting research, and addressing audiences. I have provided only a few examples of women's future visions for what writing and research in different disciplines can or could be like in the decades to come. Many more studies are needed to fully illustrate the diversity and breadth of women's commitments to change and their visions of the future of the academy (see also Minnich, *Transforming Knowledge*). If there is one theme common among women's commitments to change, it is a sense of "working against traditions," of "wanting to break the bonds of convention." And if there is one theme common to women's visions for the future of the academy, it is the desire to leave room for diversity, for multiple and multiplying visions of what it means to participate—as faculty and as students—in and across the disciplines. Minnich and her colleagues observe that "our dreams are as diverse and multihued as we. But perhaps we can say that we do not want to dream one new vision to replace the old. We recognize the danger in that. We want to open space for the dreaming of humanity, no longer forced to masquerade as "man," and a particular sort of man at that" (7).

# Portrait of a Writer: Professor Valentine
## "I see myself as a cultivator of human relationships."

Professor Valentine is an assistant professor of history and specializes in constitutional history. Like most assistant professors, she was concerned about getting tenure, but she also envisioned changes in her discipline, particularly in the kinds of writing done by historians.

THERE'S SOMETHING HEADY ABOUT MOVING BEYOND THE PH.D. and discovering that you are indeed a person within the profession, a person with power. There are these magical moments when you see something come out in print, when you see a student—students are very important to me—when you see a student go off to graduate school, achieve a master's at some wonderful university. I'm in love with the students. I think the students are utterly beyond comparison, very much in keeping with my background, too, since my background is working-class and blue-collar. In some way, you can see that you can understand them.

I went back to school when I was twenty-eight, after a career as an accountant, because we were a poor family, and I was working to keep the family in food. And so I went back to college for a B.A. and thought I was an English major because I hated history. But this marvelous history professor thought he saw a historian in me. I kept saying, "No, no, I hate history," and he kept saying, "Read this," and handed me an armful of books, and I'd go off and read these books. So he really persuaded me that there was something wonderful that I didn't know about because the history I had known before was basically high school history, taught by coaches. He was crucial; he was this very nice, gentle, soft person with pockets filled with pipes. He persuaded me. There was another person in graduate school who was similar—a facilitating, nurturing male who was not my adviser. I struck up a firm, intellectual relationship with him. I admired his mind, which moved in several dimensions all at once. I think my mind, in some ways, shaped itself after that one. He was an intellectual brain.

I went through college and graduate school with male faculty essentially. There were no women. When I left graduate school, my last year in residence, the very first woman arrived at the university. There were women beyond the academy that I admired. I think that's what happens with women; we find our female professional models elsewhere—like my mother. We know we're not like those men. My female role model is my mother. That is quite sufficient.

I always knew myself to be a better-than-average user of English, but I had very little confidence when I began graduate school. I've never penetrated that one; I don't know why there wasn't tremendous confidence when I entered graduate school. It may have to do with my latecoming to history, the fact that I was entering a discipline that was not the discipline I had planned to enter. I'm a good deal more confident now than I was even five years ago.

I did not like the fact that the dissertation, which was supposed to be mine, was in some way controlled by others. Certainly the dissertation was owned by other people in the way that I had to write for a committee, in the way that committees can pass judgment, in all of those ways. I felt that very keenly, and there was tremendous relief in getting it done. Two other women were writing dissertations, too; we formed a little group because all of us were miserable writing for other people, imagining that we had to write for other people. So we thought about it and found ways and strategies we could share with each other, to construe a certain amount of ownership.

Much of academic writing is quite bad. I'm disappointed, and have been, in fact, ever since I've been in history, about the extent to which academics have forgotten how to write and don't care about it anymore. That speaks for the part of me that once was an English major and once cared deeply about language. I also write poetry, and so I'm more aware of what it is we're doing when we sit down to write. Much of what turns out in the name of history is stringing together words. I think it's dreadful—the horrible condition of that kind of writing. It's complete irreverence for those elsewhere who might want to pick up a history book—a lack of accessibility. Much of it is pretty horrible. I want it to be good, solid English writing and not academic jargon. Those things make me sad and could be undone, especially in history. Historians have forgotten about writing.

For a junior person, I write more reviews and review essays than most. I'm also writing two articles. I've done four now, which I enjoy writing. I think articles are my favorite—no, that's not true—the class of essays is my favorite. I wish somebody would revive the essay. We don't write very many essays in history—the writing in which one simply begins and wonders where the ideas go and ends up at some destination that isn't as predictable. I seem to have managed to trick a good many journals into somehow letting me write review essays instead of book reviews. I simply present them with an essay and they are so stunned that they publish it.

But once I withdrew a long review essay from a journal. The editor changed it massively. Those weren't just minor editorial changes but major revisions. I wrote to the editor and said, "Sorry, this is mine; it is me. You will either reconsider the essay in its original form or return it." They wouldn't, so I published it elsewhere. Now that's a risk I'll take because I do not mean to go down on paper as anyone else. Oh no, I don't like predators. Minor changes are fine, but if an editor is sitting down and rewriting the entire thing, it's just not acceptable.

I can imagine writing a book of essays some day, but for now I'm trying to do what is required of me to get tenure. I'm supposed to be finishing this book, which is almost done. I'm on the last chapter. I find books more difficult to think about than essays. There is something about the notion of a very large, very complex piece of work that has to be well-integrated and well-orchestrated that initially boggles me. That's why I have to break it up into small tasks. I'm also writing an article for a magazine, which I have not done before, which is great fun. It's a different voice, and so I get to be *not* an academic. I get to speak to all those folk out there who read magazines on constitutional history. They wanted me to do an article on women in constitutionalism, so I'm doing that. I'm imagining myself as having a concrete conversation with folk who don't know as much as I do and want to learn something from me. So I'm beginning with a kind of story about a very exciting moment in the nineteenth century and then ease the reader into my mind through this storytelling procedure.

I made the rather interesting discovery lately, through writing this article, that some people actually write for good money. You enter graduate school as this normal, self-interested person who might not mind being paid for things, and you come out the other end this self-sacrificing academic prepared to do things for nothing. This magazine called me a month ago and said, "We want you to write this article on women and the Constitution. We'll pay you fifteen hundred dollars." My response was to laugh. I just howled. I started saying, "You got to be kidding. You're going to pay me fifteen hundred dollars?" You learn there are people out there who are actually getting paid for doing this thing we do for nothing. I ran around the history department giggling my head off.

I have great admiration for, great interest in, the thing that's now being called public history. I would write more for your average, ordinary, literate American, but to be absolutely frank, I need to be tenured first, because I get no credit for it. The rules were made up thirty years ago by all the chauvinistic historians who imagined that writing for the public was somehow not history. And so frankly, I intend to do this thing that's required of me, and to do it well, to enjoy it. In my book I'm going to make it just as clear as possible what I'm contributing to the profession of history. I'm going to make it as accessible as possible [to a public audience] given the constraint—the constraint being that I do, after all, have to get tenure. And I do have to get good reviews. And some day, when I am a fully empowered, tenured historian, I will do what I pretty well please, which will mean also writing for as many first-rate magazines and other kinds of publications as I can manage.

Historians typically distinguish between "narrative" on the one side, which is this cute little storytelling mode, and "analysis" on the other, which is somehow something else that historians do ever so much better. The difficulty has been dichotomization. There's no reason on earth why you can't write an analytical narrative. But they ignore all the ways in which a narrative, by definition, is analytical: narrative involves intelligence; it makes assumptions and judgments; [it] shapes itself; [it] has an engine; it explains its progress. All of those things are part of narrative, and I don't quite know why the dichotomy has to be there. The institution ought to reconsider the categories. I'm not the only one who is disgusted. There are many, many historians who can't quite understand why we are still locked into these irrational categories.

I also need to emphasize the fact that I like doing academic writing. I just know it not to be the whole job. I can imagine continuing to do academic writing and doing the other [kinds of writing]. Both are important, just very different. The language that professional historians speak is privileged in ways that literary critics talk about all the time. It's the same sort of privileged language that we may or may not be justified in speaking to one another, but by God, we have some public obligation to write history in a way that others will recognize. I wish there was more respect for the kind of history that reaches out and is read by folk at the newsstand. But historians typically don't sell books for public audiences. If you do, you risk professional delegitimization. Some day I mean to do both. I just can't yet, because one doesn't get credit. Oh, it makes me furious. I mean I'm fully prepared to go to the wall to have the rules changed. So that's the plan, to simply put myself in the position where I can do both.

There is quite a difference between public and private writing, and one is more difficult. Clearly the kind of writing we do for other professionals is much more difficult than private writing. I enjoy it once I'm doing it, but there's a certain amount of self-consciousness that I used to think was mostly female. I'm not sure about that anymore, because there are so many men that have the same sort of difficulty. The stuff I wrote even three years ago was still tainted with a certain amount of stiltedness, a certain amount of fortress-building. When I wrote my very first article, the one that ended up in print after several revisions, I remember imagining, "I have to have authority," and feeling that I didn't have it, which is why the thing ended up reading like a fortress. It was a very clear sense that someone had to establish something like my authority. I think I'm not hung up on it anymore. I've learned that authority resides wherever it is presumed to reside, and wherever it is presumed, it somehow comes through. It seems to me that one can have authority simply by knowing [one has] it, and by knowing one has it, it's no longer necessary to build a fort.

I try more and more to give over parts of my authority to my students in class and teach them about how to be an authority. But my one fear is that because of all the things we know about authority and women, it's not yet possible for us [women] to presume that kind of authority. I do find students are baffled by the fact that I don't seem to want to be terribly powerful in class. I have a certain amount of fear of abusive power, which has to do with the field I teach. I don't mean to ever, ever be accused of that kind of abuse. So you're caught just a bit, because women have to be a bit more conscious of authority and power. So I'm caught all the time between wanting to give my power away so that others can learn about it and wanting to make sure that I'm not being viewed as a powerless female. I try to give away as much authority to students as I think they can handle without viewing me simply as some version of their powerless mother, which happens every now and then. See, you've got to retain just a bit, you've got to keep just enough so that you can defend yourself against the presumption. But it's a tough spot. In writing I think it's possible simply to proceed and somehow presume that learning has its own authority. If that isn't possible, then to hell with it, because we've got to be all equals on paper. We have to be.

I have found myself writing self-consciously for my friends, because my friends are believers in conversation, and it's the conversational mode that I would prefer to adopt as I'm writing. I don't like tearing people limb from limb. I think that's kind of vicious. It's almost never necessary, and so if I mean to convey a critical point, I will do it in the course of a critical conversation, which I would like to see other historians do more often. I simply try to locate myself, to address other points of view and proceed within my own group with my position. I'm almost always able to situate myself even as I acknowledge the existence of two or three other points of view. I just frankly don't think it's necessary to win. I [want] to converse and would allow someone else to win if I could simply learn something. I'm not terribly competitive. It isn't necessary. I would prefer to just sit and write and think about history and then contribute. So I do that.

I see myself as a cultivator of human relationships, and I imagine my world as one in which relations between individuals and conversations come first. I know that's something quite foreign to a good many male colleagues who think that those kinds of interpersonal relationships have no place in the workplace. They have to be taught about it. We need a lot more folk who think that the workplace can be different. I think it's that desire to create communities that leaks over into the writing, somehow yields that nonconfrontational writing style. It may be a more loving approach to writing; there's something about wanting to converse. At conferences I view myself as having a conversation with participants and find them sometimes surprised by it and glad for it. It's about being nonconfrontational. I have no trouble making sharp criticisms, but in some fundamental way, it has to do with a lack of interest in direct, violent confrontation. I don't mean to make anybody bleed. I don't mean ever to destroy another human being through writing in a direct and violent way.

The voice is therefore, I think, a bit softer. People have told me that they find what I write refreshing because it seems less contentious, less self-consciously contentious. That, by the way, I do think is female. I'm pretty sure that's a female voice that a lot of men find quite surprising. There was a review essay I had recently written for a journal. Two of my colleagues called me up and said they were just stunned when they read this essay because by the time I was done, I had indeed shredded the book, but it was not clear until I was done that there had been a shredding.

It has been said that women are more emotionally involved in the process of writing. I think it's a very good thing. It makes it more painful sometimes. It means you're investing more of yourself, but it means that only rarely will you turn out this nonsense that looks like mechanical, hideous prose turned out without thought and loving affection. I would say that we should convert all of those folk to writing in our way, in this way that amounts to some personal investment. I've entertained the possibility that a certain love of English might be female in the way that women are statistically better writers than men and do better with language generally. I just plain love language. I don't know whether that's female, but if in fact this love of language is to some extent part of being a little girl who loved reading and loved writing and was allowed to do that because she was a little girl, then maybe it's female.

Our experiences are clearly marked by gender. I wish we could stop quibbling about our different experiences and [the different] content of our work. I wish we could just say, "Hey you guys, listen to us; we have different experiences." We could all be richer for it. I don't know when that's going to happen. It will happen when women, who insist on celebrating their experiences instead of adapting to something that doesn't work, move into positions of power. [We've] got to somehow get the women there, get the ones who have the different experiences and are not prepared to put them under a bushel, who make it rich and good and different all at once. If it happens, it ought to be interesting, because the conversation will be about different variations in academic experiences, as against *the* academic experience, which is presumed to be monolithic.

# 6

# Future Visions for Research and Teaching

DRAWING CONCLUSIONS CAN BE A TREACHEROUS ENDEAVOR, AS feminist scholars have observed. Conclusions demand that an author summarize and unify, make coherent what might be otherwise fragmented, impose order and control on material that might be otherwise out of order, out of control. Such demands can encourage researchers to reduce complex phenomena and erase differences for the sake of developing coherent—and totalizing—theories. In other words, conclusions can lead to erasing differences, and erasing differences can lead to the silencing of voices that speak "otherwise." That process, Adrienne Rich reminds us, is a powerful one: "In a world where language and naming are power, silence is oppression, is violence" (xv). It is that kind of silencing, that kind of concluding, I would like to avoid here.

Some feminist scholars have responded to the problematics of writing conclusions by offering no conclusions (e.g., Flax, *Thinking Fragments: Psychoanalysis, Feminism, and Postmodernism in the Contemporary West*) or by offering multiple conclusions (e.g., Lather, *Getting Smart: Feminist Research and Pedagogy With/in the Postmodern*). I begin this conclusion by noting that the women I interviewed are *not* meant to be representative—and therefore cannot lend justification to broad generalizations. I am not able to—nor would I want to—make definitive claims about "women's writing experiences" or "women's academic experiences." Instead, this study explored how *some* women—successful students and faculty members—in *some* disciplines and in *one* setting talked about their work—how they narrated their intellectual lives. Specifically, the study examined the ways these women reported going about their writing and research, about establishing their authority and address-ing the authority of their readers. Their stories are meant to provide a glimpse of the range of issues academic women are likely to face in their work and the diverse ways they respond to those issues. To that effect, this study is partly descriptive, giving space and voice to different women's experiences. The portraits of writers between chapters, for example, present women's narrations without interrup-tion or analysis, thereby allowing women's voices to become audible. In this respect, I have followed one the feminist research principles described by Susan Geiger in her discussion of oral histories: "[In-terviews] accept women's own interpretations of their identities, their experiences, and social worlds as containing and reflecting im-portant truths, and do not categorize and, therefore, dismiss them, for the purposes of generalization, as *simply* subjective" (170; Gei-er's emphasis).

Women's descriptions of their writing and research activities are also meant to bring attention to the social, cultural, and political dimensions that shape writing and academic life. Gender is one point of departure—among many possible ones—for examining the contexts that shape writing, just as it is one aspect of lived experi-ence that can shape identity (among many others). We know that gender is a critical issue throughout the entire educational process, as the recent report by the American Association of University Women (AAUW) documents. Focusing on elementary and second-ary education, the AAUW report suggests that "girls encounter first grade with the same or better skills and ambitions as boys. But, all too often, by the time they finish high school, 'their doubts have crowded out their dreams'" (qtd. in Kantrowitz et al. 62). Since this pattern of "downward intellectual mobility" (62) emerges in early education, it is not surprising to find it continues as women pursue higher education and enter academic careers.

Although the women I interviewed were successful faculty mem-bers and students who had created places for themselves in the academy, their sense of authority remained fragile. For example, a full professor of history observed that the "stereotypical reaction to a female never goes away, even after years and years of experiences and credentials"; and an assistant professor of history remembered losing her self-confidence during graduate school: "I always knew myself to be a better-than-average user of English, but I had very little confidence when I began graduate school"; and a returning graduate student in anthropology reported on the "terror" and fear of writing she had experienced during her first two years in graduate school: "I have found the writing part of graduate school terrifying. . . . I hit an all-time low in the first year of graduate school when I received such harsh criticism on my writing. . . . It made me totally insecure. It blew out everything that I had tried to do"; and an undergraduate student in education reported that once she got to college, she discovered there were better writers: "I'm not as good a writer as I thought I was. When I was in high school, I could write circles around everybody. But . . . once I got into college, there were better writers." These comments remind us that women's confidence is not to be taken for granted at any level of the educational process or in the academic career path; they illustrate what the AAUW report confirms: that women's educational advancement does not always correlate with a growth in confidence.

Furthermore, this study suggests that as women advance along the academic ranks, issues of authority can become more—rather than less—pronounced. Predominantly women faculty members, rather than the students, reported on strategies for achieving distance from their writing and from academic audiences (discussed in chapter 3), on their commitment to changing the nature of academic writing and the audiences it reaches (discussed in chapter 4), and on the nonmainstream or interdisciplinary nature of their work (discussed in chapter 5). Taken together, these factors complicate positions of authority for women. While I have discussed issues of audience, authority, and transformation separately in the different chapters (for convenience's sake), it should be clear by now that they are closely intertwined. For example, women who are crossing disciplinary boundaries to ask new research questions are likely to question the traditions of their home disciplines, likely to expand the audiences for whom they write, and likely to change the kinds of writing they do—all of which call into question their authority as members of the academy.

Women in both male- and female-dominated fields reported that establishing authority remained a continued concern at various points throughout their careers. A full professor working in history, a fairly male-dominated field, noted: "[For women], any kind of flavor or personality or opinion or extra style will be reacted to negatively. I've had that experience. The pressure is for you to be so in lockstep with the system that there is assurance that you can be controlled." And an associate professor in nursing, a discipline where the percentage of women faculty members is high, explained:

> In a lot of institutions of higher education, the school of nursing is under the school of medicine—either literally or figuratively. Either the structure is such that the school of nursing is under medicine or the school of nursing is dominated by it. . . . Nursing has a . . . gender issue with medicine, that traditional power structure has gone along gender lines. In academia there are also gender issues around the prestigious units in the university. They are generally male-dominated. And the less prestigious units, like social work, like education, like nursing, are more female-dominated. So you definitely feel that.

In this study, then, women *across* disciplines and academic ranks—faculty members in particular—reported that they encountered challenges to their authority at least some of the time. As Minnich, O'Barr, and Rosenfeld caution,

> We may be in the academy; we may be bringing feminist scholarship into the curriculum; we may be changing ways of teaching and working; but that does not mean we have eliminated the sex/ gender hierarchy. It is expressed in sexual harassment just as it was in our exclusion, and both reduce us to our male-defined bodies. Again we are reminded that even our physical presence in the academy is a profound challenge to the dominant tradition. Simply by being there, we are seen as provocative. Achieving access is not, cannot be, enough. (5)

However, it is also important to remember that all women who participated in this study were *successful* faculty members and students as well as prolific writers. They had managed to participate in, and contribute to, academic scholarship across the ranks and disciplines. Students were above-average performers and strong writers; faculty members had long, successful careers and enjoyed professional recognition as members of their disciplines. These women had success-fully entered the academy and at the same time found avenues to begin realizing their visions for change.

Taking into account that most women's lives are complicated by their roles as primary caregivers, mothers, and wives, their accom-plishments are all the more noteworthy. In this study, I did not examine the conditions under which women work and live, al-though it is evident that those conditions have profound effects on the quality of women's lives and on their abilities to pursue an edu-cation or academic career. As a returning graduate student in an-thropology described: "We [women] are trying to deal with all the responsibilities that we have. . . . We have two jobs. I think a lot of us are dealing with home situations that take a lot of energy." Those responsibilities are critical to women's success—or failure—in the academy, as we are reminded by Aisenberg and Harrington:

> Given the relentless pressure of time, the necessity to compress two days, two lives into one, the most serious threat to women's superhuman effort at integration [of their personal and profes-sional lives] is encountering unforeseen trouble. . . . The point is that women have so little margin, they operate so close to the bone, that it just takes [one] extra burden to break the personal/professional synthesis to pieces. (121)

Or, in the words of Patricia Ireland, president of the National Or-ganization for Women, "Women are stretched within an inch of their lives" (qtd. in Beyette E1).

In her reflections on the women's movement, Ellen Goodman notes that women have set for themselves at least two tasks: to gain access to institutions and to transform them. So far, Goodman notes, women have only succeeded with the first task: "The reality is that the women's movement stood on two legs. With one, we kicked open the doors. With the other we were to change the system. But the second is still dragging way behind the first. . . . Women have gained access to the institutions, but not enough power to overhaul them" (B7). That then—the task of overhauling the institution—is the challenge women in the academy have set for themselves. Women in this study described many different visions of changing the nature of their research, their writing, and their disciplines;

their visions were as diverse as the challenges they faced were far-reaching. These women were engaged in transforming all facets of the academy, a process that demands courage, vision, and commitment. Minnich and her colleagues remind us that "we speak here of re-creating a whole tradition, a whole culture, polity, world" (7). The challenge of this study—like that in the collection of essays, *Women Teachers: Issues and Experiences*—is "to the nature of authority it-self. It is not so much about putting women in positions of power as about the need for both men and women to insist on a new balance of values wherever power is being exercised" (Benn xix). That kind of "new balance of values" is at the heart of women's visions for transforming the academy.

One important aspect of women's visions lies in transforming the teaching that goes on in institutions of higher education. Feminist scholars have long observed that the classroom climate is a "chilly one" for women as well as other marginalized groups (e.g., Hall; Spender and Sarah; Simeone). Frey, for example, notes how perva-sive the competitive environment is throughout higher education: "I see the adversary method in our pedagogy and classroom struc-tures, in our faculty meetings, in the formats of our conferences, in informal encounters in the hall, in every corner of our public lives. The adversary method is only a symptom of a pervading ethos that stresses competition and individualistic achievement at the expense of connectedness to others" (522). Scholars like Frey are urging us to envision new ways of teaching, writing, and creating knowledge, and a variety of feminist pedagogies are now being developed to warm the chilly climate for women. New pedagogical approaches vary from introducing "maternal thinking" (Lamb, "Minimizing Es-sentialism") to an "ethic of care" (Schweickart) to "midwife teach-ers" (Belenky et al.) to "sophistic rhetoric" (Jarratt). I will not at-tempt to review the many new and innovative pedagogies here; several books and journals are devoted to the topic (see, e.g., Goetsch's annotated bibliography on feminist pedagogy in the *Na-tional Women's Studies Association Journal*; the special issues of the *Journal of Advanced Composition* ["Gender, Culture, and Ide-ology," Fall 1990] and *Women's Studies Quarterly* [Women, Girls, and the Culture of Education," Spring/Summer 1991]; and books on the topics such as Gabriel and Smithson, *Gender in the Classroom: Power and Pedagogy* and Weiler, *Women Teaching for Change: Gender, Class, and Power*).

The many emerging feminist pedagogies have at least one common denominator: their opposition to educational environments that stress competition and individual achievement over cooperation and collaborative work. Belenky and her colleagues, for example, have proposed a model of education that emphasizes a sense of community and "connected knowing" over competition and "separate knowing" (190–213). Writing teachers have begun to incorporate aspects of this model into their teaching through such methods as collaborative writing groups, peer feedback, and portfolio evaluations.

However, a feminist pedagogy cannot abandon argument and debate or ignore competition altogether. Lamb notes that "we can't afford not to teach students to argue well, but where we can make a difference is in what the arguing is for and at what point it comes in the whole process of responding to conflict" (Letter). If feminist teachers and students hope to change education, the academy, and society at large, they must be able to argue forcefully, with conviction, in places where decisions are made that can affect their lives. Steinitz and Kantor express a similar point about the limitations of Belenky et al.'s model of connected education:

> Connected education is an appealing model. Certainly it promotes positive values—affirming rather than attacking those with whom one disagrees, searching for areas of consensus rather than accentuating differences, and collaborating for the sake of collective learning rather than competing in order to demonstrate one's own superiority. Yet it has its limits. Encouraging women to *find* their own voices must be followed by challenging women to develop the confidence and courage to *use* their voices—to speak up at home and work, question authorities, and fight for what they believe is right. (139; Steinitz and Kantor's emphasis)

I quote Steinitz and Kantor's critique not to diminish the importance of Belenky et al.'s work; their research has made an important contribution to theories of education and has become an impetus for change that has inspired educators, composition teachers, and feminist scholars alike. Rather, I cite Steinitz and Kantor as an important reminder that we need to explore a variety of pedagogical approaches, that we need to encourage all our students—women *and* men—to find occasions for collaboration and consensus-building while, at the same time, teaching them the skills of how and when to be assertive, how and when to claim authority.

Two faculty members in this study reported that they had explored alternative approaches to teaching; one had experimented with allowing students to become authorities in the classroom:

> I try more and more to give over parts of my authority to my students in class and teach them about how to be an authority. But my one fear is that because of all the things we know about authority and women, it's not yet possible for us [women] to presume that kind of authority. I do find students are baffled by the fact that I don't seem to want to be terribly powerful in class. . . . I try to give away as much authority to students as I think they can handle without viewing me simply as some version of their powerless mother, which happens every now and then. See, you've got to retain just a bit, you've got to keep just enough so that you can defend yourself against the presumption. (An assistant professor of history)

This professor, familiar with the feminist discourse on pedagogy and power, understands the limitations of her approach to teaching: that her willingness to share or "give away" authority might be misunderstood, perhaps even abused, by students. As Benn reminds us, "Historically, there have always been two distinct teaching functions: the first an extension of mothering, and reserved for women; the second an extension of power and authority, reserved for men, who have guarded it well" (xix). Women in higher education are often caught between these two teaching functions; while they are authorities in their fields, students often fail to perceive them as such and expect them to act in more stereotypical female roles—for example, in supportive and nurturing capacities (see also Bauer; Jarratt; and Simeone for discussions of the often troubling responses students bring to female teachers, particularly feminist teachers).

Another woman I interviewed, a doctoral student in nursing who worked as a full-time lecturer, reflected on what she considered another important pedagogical goal: to listen to students' experiences—in her case, practicing nurses—and encourage them to write about their experiences:

Nurses should be encouraged to write more often. There are a lot of nurses who have some wonderful ideas and tremendous experiences, and there's very little out there that's written about those experiences. I wonder if nurses don't write less than a lot of other professionals. Maybe it's because we're so busy taking care of patients, because we're so exhausted. But I wonder if we as faculty aren't too negative; I think our academic system can be real negative. . . . I wonder how many people we lose because we've made it so competitive.

It is exactly this kind of change—a move *away* from competition and *toward* building connections between lived experience and academic subject matters—that educators like Belenky et al. advocate in their model of connected education. By inviting students to begin collecting their own personal narratives as well as those of friends and colleagues, as this teacher of nursing suggests, we allow students to recognize the validity of their own experiences and encourage them to take control of their educational processes.

To further allow women to take control of their education, we must alert them to the possible challenges to their authority that they can face as they pursue their education and enter academic career paths. Such teaching would include a discussion of the various social factors—gender, race, and class among them—that shape rhetorical situations and that can contribute to who will be recognized as an authority and whose utterances will be considered authoritative. We *cannot* change the fact that gender is, at least to some degree, a critical factor in rhetorical situations, but we *can* educate women about the challenges to their authority that they are likely to encounter. We can also educate them about the courage, wisdom, and commitment of other academic women as well as about the innovative and diverse strategies for addressing issues of authority that other women have developed. Such knowledge would allow women to focus their energies on their work, not on inventing new ways of establishing their authority every time it is challenged; it would allow them to discover a sense of community and tradition among academic women who have traveled the road ahead. Rich describes the importance of such traditions: "For if, in trying to join the common world of men, the professions molded by a primarily masculine consciousness, we split ourselves off from the common life of women and deny our female heritage and identity in our work, we [women] lose touch with our real powers and with the essential condition for all fully realized work: community" (xv). Such teaching would also introduce students to the range of women's visions for changing the academy. In this study, all faculty members and some students expressed the desire to address a wide range of public audiences, to transform and expand academic kinds of writing, and to engage in interdisciplinary or nonmainstream work. Bringing those visions into the classroom would prepare women for the challenges ahead and would enable them to participate in transforming research and scholarship across the disciplines. By teaching students how to address diverse audiences, for example, including nonacademic ones, we would not only bring attention to the limited types of discourse usually produced and valued in the university, but we would also enrich *all* students' sense of audience. By teaching students how scholars establish authority and create knowledge, we would not only demystify the making of knowledge across the disciplines, but we would also enable *all* students to participate actively in their education and in the academic enterprise. Finally, by showing students that disciplinary boundaries are provisional and changing, we would invite ingenuity and encourage creativity.

In the spirit of Harding, who suggests that research studies might best serve to raise questions, not lead to conclusions, I end this book by listing a number of questions that are critical for the future of women's education and academic career paths: How can we prepare women to gain the authority it takes to speak as professionals as well as the confidence it takes to study new research topics and explore new forms of discourse? How can we broaden our definitions of academic discourse and allow scholars—both men and women—to write in diverse genres for diverse audiences? How can we ensure that diversity in writing and research is valued in institutional and professional communities across the disciplines? How can we ensure that women who engage in nonmainstream or interdisciplinary work establish their authority in the academy? Finally, how can we redefine existing disciplinary boundaries to make room for the kind of work in which women—and an increasing number of men—are likely to engage? These questions are vital to women's daily lives as scholars and teachers. At stake is nothing less than a new vision of what constitutes reading and writing—our scholarly work—in the academy.

Appendix
Works Cited and Consulted

# Appendix

First Interview Questions

    The questions I will ask you are meant to help me learn more about your experience as a writer and as a woman in the academic setting. There are no right or wrong answers. I am interested in all aspects of your experience. Let me first ask you a few questions about your educational and professional experiences.

1. *Faculty:* How long have you been at this university and how did you get here?
   *Students:* What made you decide to go to college/graduate school at this university?
2. *Faculty:* Where did you complete your graduate education? Did you teach at other institutions before coming to this university?
   *Students:* Where did you complete your high school/undergraduate education?
3. What has your experience at this university been like since you came here? Has it been different than or just like you expected it to be?
4. *Faculty:* What is working in your department like? How do you fit into your department?
   *Students:* What do you think you'll remember about your educational experience at this university five years from now?
5. *Faculty:* Does the proportion of male and female colleagues in this department make a difference to your work and productivity?
   *Students:* Does the proportion of male and female students in your field of study make a difference to your work and productivity?
6. *Faculty:* Looking back over the last five years of your professional life, what are some of the high and low points?

*Students*: Looking back over the last few years of your educational experience, what are some of the high and low points?

7. Is there someone you consider to be your role model or mentor?

Now I would like to ask you about your writing experiences:

8. What comes to mind for you when you think about academic writing? What are your first thoughts and reactions?
9. *Faculty*: Tell me about the writing you typically do in your professional life. I am interested in anything from memos and conference presentations to research articles and book projects.
   *Students*: Tell me about the writing you have been asked to do in college/graduate school. I am interested in anything from notes to essays, research papers, and articles.
10. What writing projects are you working on this semester?
11. *Students*: You have just told me about the writing you do *in* the university. Is there also writing you do outside the university context, such as writing letters to friends, keeping a diary, writing poetry, or writing on the job?
12. From all the writing you just named, which kinds do you prefer? Why?
13. From all the writing you just named, which kinds are the most difficult for you? Why?
14. What kinds of readers do you write for? How do you address these readers? What do you imagine readers to be like?
15. Do you ever feel that you have to write for conflicting audiences? If so, how do you address these conflicting audiences?
16. How would you describe your "voice" in writing, the way you come across or would like to come across? Do you feel that you have to take on a certain persona to write successful academic papers?
17. How do you establish your authority in your writing?
18. Have there been writing situations when you found it difficult to establish your authority? If so, why?
19. Is ownership of the text ever an issue for you? Do you feel that you own or control your writing or that others own and control it?
20. Do you consider yourself a confident writer? Sometimes? All the time?
21. Has your sense of yourself as a writer changed over time? How so?
22. Do you think that being a woman influences your writing experience? If so, how?
23. Tell me about your writing habits. How do you go about writing? How often do you write? For what length of time do you write? In what environment do you like to write?

24. What kind of feedback do you get or would you like to get while you are writing? Are there people you show your work-in-progress and finished writing to?

25. Do you have any memorable stories related to your writing experiences, good or bad? Please tell me about them.

26. Now that you have done some reflecting on your writing experiences, is there anything else you would like to add?

## Second Interview Questions

1. Did you have any further thoughts on the nature of your writing and research experiences since our last conversation?

Last time I asked whether you would be willing to discuss a current piece of writing with me today. Let me ask you a few questions about the piece of writing you have chosen to talk about:

2. What was the goal and purpose of this piece of writing? How well do you think you accomplished these goals?

3. *Faculty*: Who are the readers for this piece? How did you address them?
   *Students*: Who are the readers for this piece? How did you address them? If you could pick an audience for this piece other than your instructor, who would you write it for? Would you write the piece differently? How so?

4. How would you describe your tone and voice in this piece? Is there a certain role or persona you assume?

5. How did the piece evolve and develop over time? What changes did you make and why?

6. Were some aspects of this piece particularly easy or difficult to write? Why?

7. How satisfied are you with this piece? Please explain.

8. Do you have any other comments about writing this piece?

Now a few broader questions:

9. Do you ever try to reach a broader audience, one that goes beyond the immediate academic audience, in your writing?

10. *Faculty*: Do you consider your work to be typical or atypical of your discipline? That is, do you consider your work to be inside or outside the mainstream of your discipline? What makes it so?

*Students*: Do you consider your thesis to be typical or atypical of your major/field of study? That is, do you consider your work to be inside or outside the mainstream of your major/field? What makes it so?

11. *Faculty*: What advice would you give to graduate students in your discipline about succeeding in graduate school and in academic careers?
*Students*: What advice would you give to other students in your field about succeeding in college/graduate school?

12. *Faculty*: What advice would you give to graduate students about keys to successful writing and research in your field?
*Students*: What advice would you give to other students about keys to successful writing and research in your field?

# Works Cited and Consulted

Aisenberg, Nadya, and Mona Harrington. *Women of Academe: Outsiders in the Sacred Grove.* Amherst: U of Massachusetts P, 1988.

Alcoff, Linda. "Cultural Feminism versus Poststructuralism: The Identity Crisis in Feminist Theory." *Reconstructing the Academy: Women's Education and Women's Studies.* Ed. Elizabeth Minnich, Jean O'Barr, and Rachel Rosenfeld. Chicago: U of Chicago P, 1988. 257–88.

Annas, Pamela. "Style as Politics: A Feminist Approach to the Teaching of Writing." *College English* 47 (1985): 360–71.

Ashton-Jones, Evelyn, and Dene Kay Thomas. "Composition, Collaboration, and Women's Ways of Knowing: A Conversation with Mary Belenky." *Journal of Advanced Composition* 10 (1990): 275–92.

Barthes, Roland. "The Death of the Author." *Image-Music-Text.* Trans. Stephen Heath. New York: Hill and Wang, 1977. 142–48.

Bartholomae, David. "Inventing the University." *When a Writer Can't Write: Studies in Writer's Block.* Ed. Mike Rose. New York: Guilford, 1985. 134–65.

Bateson, Mary C. *Composing A Life.* New York: Plume, 1990.

Bauer, Dale. "Authority: Feminist Bywords." *National Women's Studies Association Journal* 3 (1991): 95–97.

Bazerman, Charles. "What Written Knowledge Does: Three Examples of Academic Discourse." *Philosophy of the Social Sciences* 11 (1981): 361–87.

Belenky, Mary, Blythe Clinchy, Nancy Goldberger, and Jill Tarule. *Women's Ways of Knowing: The Development of Self, Voice, and Mind.* New York: Basic, 1986.

Benn, Caroline. Introduction. *Women Teachers: Issues and Experiences.* Ed. Hilary de Lyon and Frances Migniuolo. Philadelphia: Open UP, 1989. xix–xxvi.

Berkenkotter, Carol. "Student Writers and Their Sense of Authority over Texts." *College Composition and Communication* 35 (1984): 312–19.

Berkenkotter, Carol, Thomas Huckin, and John Ackerman. "Conventions, Conversations, and the Writer: Case Study of a Student in a Rhetoric Ph.D. Program." *Research in the Teaching of English* 22 (1988): 9–44.

Berlin, James A. *Rhetoric and Reality: Writing Instruction in American Colleges, 1900–1985.* Carbondale: Southern Illinois UP, 1987.

Bernard, Jessie. *Academic Women.* 2d ed. New York: NAL, 1974.

Beyette, Beverly. "Then and NOW." *Los Angeles Times* 24 Feb. 1992: E1–2.

Bizzell, Patricia. "What Happens When Basic Writers Come to College?" *College Composition and Communication* 37 (1986): 294–301.

Bleich, David. "Genders of Writing." *Journal of Advanced Composition* 9 (1989): 10–25.

Bloom, Allan. *The Closing of the American Mind: How Higher Education Has Failed Democracy and Impoverished the Souls of Today's Students.* New York: Simon, 1987.

Bloom, Lynn. "Why Don't We Write What We Teach? And Publish It?" *Journal of Advanced Composition* 10 (1990): 87–100.

Boice, Robert, and Kelly A. Kelly. "Writing Viewed by Disenfranchised Groups: A Study of Women and Women's College Faculty." *Written Communication* 4 (1987): 299–309.

Brodkey, Linda. *Academic Writing as Social Practice.* Philadelphia: Temple UP, 1987.

———. "Writing Ethnographic Narratives." *Written Communication* 4 (1987): 25–50.

Brodzki, Bella, and Celeste Schenck. Introduction. *Life/Lines: Theorizing Women's Autobiography.* Ed. Brodzki and Schenck. Ithaca: Cornell UP, 1988. 1–15.

Brooke, Robert, and John Hendricks. *Audience Expectations and Teacher Demands.* Carbondale: Southern Illinois UP, 1989.

Bruffee, Kenneth A. "Social Construction, Language, and the Authority of Knowledge: A Bibliographical Essay." *College English* 48 (1986): 773–90.

Bullock, Richard, and John Trimbur, eds. *The Politics of Writing Instruction: Postsecondary.* Portsmouth, NH: Boynton Cook, 1991.

Cayton, Mary Kupiec. "What Happens When Things Go Wrong: Women and Writing Blocks." *Journal of Advanced Composition* 10 (1990): 321–37.

Caywood, Cynthia, and Gillian Overing, eds. *Teaching Writing: Pedagogy, Gender, and Equity.* Albany: State U of New York P, 1987.

Chamberlain, Miriam K., ed. *Women in Academe: Progress and Prospects.* New York: Russell Sage Foundation, 1988.

Chase, Susan E. "Making Sense of 'The Woman Who Becomes a Man.'" *Gender and Discourse: The Power of Talk.* Ed. Alexandra Dundas Todd and Sue Fisher. Norwood, NJ: Ablex, 1988. 275–95.

Chesler, Phyllis. *Women and Madness.* Garden City: Doubleday, 1972.

Clark, Beverly Lyon, and Sonja Wiedenhaupt. "On Blocking and Unblocking Sonja: A Case Study in Two Voices." *College Composition and Communication* 43 (1992): 55–74.

Clark, Suzanne. *Sentimental Modernism: Women Writers and the Revolution of the Word.* Bloomington: Indiana UP, 1991.

Coates, Jennifer. *Women, Men, and Language: A Sociolinguistic Account of Sex Differences in Language.* New York: Longman, 1986.

Coates, Jennifer, and Deborah Cameron, eds. *Women in Their Speech Communities: New Perspectives on Language and Sex.* New York: Longman, 1988.

De Lauretis, Teresa. "The Essence of the Triangle or, Taking the Risk of Essentialism Seriously: Feminist Theory in Italy, the U.S., and Britain." *Differences: A Journal of Feminist Cultural Studies* 1 (1989): 3–37.

DuBois, Ellen C., Gail P. Kelly, Elizabeth L. Kennedy, Carolyn W. Korsmeyer, and Lillian S. Robinson. *Feminist Scholarship: Kindling in the Groves of Academe.* Urbana: U of Illinois P, 1985.

Ede, Lisa, and Andrea Lunsford. "Audience Addressed/Audience Invoked: The Role of Audience in Composition Theory and Pedagogy." *College Composition and Communication* 35 (1984): 155–71.

Elbow, Peter. "Closing My Eyes as I Speak: An Argument for Ignoring Audience." *College English* 49 (1987): 50–69.

———. "Reflections on Academic Discourse: How It Relates to Freshmen and Colleagues." *College English* 53 (1991): 135–55.

Elgin, Suzette Haden. *Native Tongue.* London: Women's Press, 1985.

Farnham, Christie, ed. *The Impact of Feminist Research in the Academy.* Bloomington: Indiana UP, 1987.

Ferguson, Kathy E. "Subject-centredness in Feminist Discourse." *The Po-*

*litical Interests of Gender: Developing Theory and Research with a Feminist Face*. Ed. Kathleen B. Jones and Anna G. Jonasdottir. Newbury Park, CA: Sage, 1988. 66–78.

Fetterly, Judith. *The Resisting Reader: A Feminist Approach to American Fiction*. Bloomington: Indiana UP, 1978.

Fish, Stanley. "Being Interdisciplinary Is So Very Hard to Do." *Profession 89*. Ed. Phyllis Franklin. New York: MLA, 1989. 15–22.

Fishman, Pamela. "Conversational Insecurity." *The Feminist Critique of Language*. Ed. Deborah Cameron. New York: Routledge, 1990. 234–41.

Flax, Jane. *Thinking Fragments: Psychoanalysis, Feminism, and Postmodernism in the Contemporary West*. Berkeley: U of California P, 1990.

Flower, Linda, and John R. Hayes. "The Cognition of Discovery: Defining a Rhetorical Problem." *College Composition and Communication* 31 (1980): 21–32.

Flynn, Elizabeth. "Composing as a Woman." *College Composition and Communication* 39 (1988): 423–35.

———. "Composing 'Composing as a Woman.'" *College Composition and Communication* 41 (1990): 83–89.

———. "Composing Difference: Toward an Epistemology of Presence." Conference on College Composition and Communication. Cincinnati, 20 Mar. 1992.

Flynn, Elizabeth, and Patrocinio Schweickart, eds. *Gender and Reading: Essays on Readers, Texts, and Contexts*. Baltimore: John Hopkins UP, 1986.

Fonow, Mary Margaret, and Judith Cook. *Beyond Methodology: Feminist Scholarship as Lived Research*. Bloomington: Indiana UP, 1991.

Frank, Francine, and Frank Anshen. *Language and the Sexes*. Albany: State U of New York P, 1983.

Frey, Olivia. "Beyond Literary Darwinism: Women's Voices and Critical Discourse." *College English* 52 (1990): 507–26.

Fuss, Diana. *Essentially Speaking: Feminism, Nature, and Difference*. New York: Routledge, 1989.

———. "Reading Like a Feminist." *Differences: A Journal of Feminist Cultural Studies* 1 (1989): 77–92.

Gabriel, Susan L., and Isaiah Smithson, eds. *Gender in the Classroom: Power and Pedagogy*. Urbana: U of Illinois P, 1990.

Gardiner, Judith Kegan. "On Female Identity and Writing by Women."

*Writing and Sexual Difference.* Ed. Elizabeth Abel. Chicago: U of Chicago P, 1982. 177–91.

Geiger, Susan. "What's So Feminist About Women's Oral History?" *Journal of Women's History* 2 (1990): 169–82.

Geisler, Cheryl. "Exploring Academic Literacy: An Experiment in Composing." *College Composition and Communication* 43 (1992): 39–54.

Gere, Anne Ruggles. *Writing Groups: History, Theory, and Implications.* Carbondale: Southern Illinois UP, 1987.

Gilligan, Carol. *In a Different Voice: Psychological Theory and Women's Development.* Cambridge, MA: Harvard UP, 1982.

Goetsch, Lori. "Feminist Pedagogy: A Selective Annotated Bibliography." *National Women's Studies Association Journal* 3 (1991): 422–29.

Goodman, Ellen. "Time for a Second Generation Change." *Los Angeles Times* 25 Feb. 1992: B7.

Graff, Gerald. *Professing Literature: An Institutional History.* Chicago: U of Chicago P, 1987.

Hall, Roberta, with Bernice Sandler. *The Classroom Climate: A Chilly One for Women?* Washington, DC: Project on the Status and Education of Women, Assn. of American Colleges, 1982.

Harding, Sandra. "Is There a Feminist Method?" *Feminism and Methodology: Social Science Issues.* Ed. Harding. Bloomington: Indiana UP, 1987. 1–14.

Heilbrun, Carolyn G. "The Politics of Mind." *Gender in the Classroom: Power and Pedagogy.* Ed. Susan L. Gabriel and Isaiah Smithson. Urbana: U of Illinois P, 1990. 28–40.

Herron, Jerry. *Universities and the Myth of Cultural Decline.* Detroit: Wayne State UP, 1988.

Hillocks, George. *Research on Written Composition: New Directions for Teaching.* Urbana, IL: NCRE and ERIC, 1986.

Horowitz, Helen Lefkowitz. *Alma Mater: Design and Experience in the Women's Colleges from their Nineteenth-Century Beginnings to the 1930s.* New York: Knopf, 1984.

Irigaray, Luce. "Equal to Whom?" *Differences: A Journal of Feminist Cultural Studies* 1 (1989): 59–76.

Jarratt, Susan. "Feminism and Composition: The Case for Conflict." *Contending With Words: Composition and Rhetoric in a Postmodern Age.* Ed. Patricia Harkin and John Schilb. New York: MLA, 1991. 105–23.

Jones, Kathleen. "On Authority: Or, Why Women Are Not Entitled to

Speak." *Authority Revisited.* Ed. J. Roland Pennock and John W. Chapman. New York: New York UP, 1987. 152–68.

———. "The Trouble With Authority." *Differences: A Journal of Feminist Cultural Studies* 3 (1991): 104–27.

Jones, Kathleen B., and Anna G. Jonasdottir. "Gender as an Analytical Category." *The Political Interests of Gender: Developing Theory and Research with a Feminist Face.* Ed. Jones and Jonasdottir. Newbury Park, CA: Sage, 1988. 1–10.

Kantrowitz, Barbara, Pat Wingert, and Patrick Houston. "Sexism in the Schoolhouse." *Newsweek* 24 Feb. 1992: 62.

Kirsch, Gesa. "Experienced Writers' Sense of Audience and Authority: Three Case Studies." *A Sense of Audience in Written Communication.* Ed. Kirsch and Duane Roen. Newbury Park, CA: Sage, 1990. 216–30.

———. "Methodological Pluralism: Epistemological Issues." *Methods and Methodology in Composition Research.* Ed. Kirsch and Patricia A. Sullivan. Carbondale: Southern Illinois UP, 1992. 247–69.

———. "Writing Up and Down the Social Ladder: A Study of Experienced Writers Composing for Contrasting Audiences." *Research in the Teaching of English* 25 (1991): 33–53.

Kohlberg, Lawrence. "Moral Stages and Moralization: The Cognitive-Developmental Approach." *Moral Development and Behavior.* Ed. T. Lickona. New York: Holt, 1976. 31–53.

Kramarae, Cheris, and Paula Treichler. *A Feminist Dictionary.* London: Pandora, 1985.

Lakoff, Robin. "Extract from *Language and Woman's Place.*" *The Feminist Critique of Language.* Ed. Deborah Cameron. New York: Routledge, 1990. 221–33.

Lamb, Catherine. "Beyond Argument in Feminist Composition." *College Composition and Communication* 42 (1991): 11–24.

———. Letter to the author. 19 May 1992.

———. "Minimizing Essentialism: Maternal Thinking and Writer/Reader Relationships." Conference on College Composition and Communication. Cincinnati, 20 Mar. 1992.

Langellier, Kristin, and Deanna Hall. "Interviewing Women: A Phenomenological Approach to Feminist Communication Research." *Doing Research on Women's Communication: Perspectives on Theory and Method.* Ed. Kathryn Carter and Carole Spitzack. Norwood, NJ: Ablex, 1989. 193–220.

Lather, Patricia. *Getting Smart: Feminist Research and Pedagogy With/in the Postmodern.* New York: Routledge, 1991.

Lie, Suzanne Stiver, and Virginia O'Leary, eds. *Storming the Tower: Women in the Academic World.* London: Kogan Page, 1990.

Long, Russell. "Writer-Audience Relationship: Analysis or Invention?" *College Composition and Communication* 31 (1980): 221–26.

Lowe, Marian, and Ruth Hubbard, eds. *Woman's Nature: Rationalizations of Inequality.* New York: Pergamon, 1982.

MacDonald, Susan Peck. "Problem Definition in Academic Writing." *College English* 49 (1987): 315–31.

———. *Professional Academic Writing in the Humanities and Social Sciences.* Carbondale: Southern Illinois UP, forthcoming.

McQuade, Donald. "Living in—and on—the Margins." *College Composition and Communication* 43 (1992): 11–22.

Miller, Carolyn, and Jack Selzer. "Special Topics of Argument in Engineering Reports." *Writing in Nonacademic Settings.* Ed. Lee Odell and Dixie Goswami. New York: Guilford, 1985. 309–41.

Miller, Nancy K. "Changing the Subject: Authorship, Writing, and the Reader." *Feminist Studies/Critical Studies.* Ed. Teresa de Lauretis. Bloomington: Indiana UP, 1986. 102–20.

Miller, Susan. *Rescuing the Subject: A Critical Introduction to Rhetoric and the Writer.* Carbondale: Southern Illinois UP, 1989.

Minnich, Elizabeth. *Transforming Knowledge.* Philadelphia: Temple UP, 1990.

Minnich, Elizabeth, Jean O'Barr, and Rachel Rosenfeld. Introduction. *Reconstructing the Academy: Women's Education and Women's Studies.* Ed. Minnich, O'Barr, and Rosenfeld. Chicago: U of Chicago P, 1988. 1–8.

Mitchell, Ruth, and Mary Taylor. "The Integrating Perspective: An Audience-Response Model for Writing." *College English* 41 (1979): 247–71.

Moran, Charles. "A Life in the Profession." *An Introduction to Composition Studies.* Ed. Erika Lindemann and Gary Tate. New York: Oxford UP, 1991. 160–82.

Nelson, Jenny L. "Phenomenology as Feminist Methodology: Explicating Interviews." *Doing Research on Women's Communication: Perspectives on Theory and Method.* Ed. Kathryn Carter and Carole Spitzack. Norwood, NJ: Ablex, 1989. 221–43.

Nicholson, Linda, ed. *Feminism/Postmodernism.* New York: Routledge, 1990.

Oakley, Ann. "Interviewing Women: A Contradiction in Terms." *Doing Feminist Research.* Ed. Helen Roberts. New York: Routledge, 1981. 30–61.

Oates, Mary J., and Susan Williamson. "Women's Colleges and Women Achievers." *Signs: Journal of Women in Culture and Society* 3 (1978): 795–806.

Olsen, Tillie. *Silences.* New York: Delta/Bantam Doubleday, 1978.

Ong, Walter. "The Writer's Audience is Always a Fiction." *Publications of the Modern Language Association* 90 (1975): 6–21.

Park, Douglas. "Analyzing Audiences." *College Composition and Communication* 37 (1986): 478–88.

———. "The Meanings of 'Audience.'" *College English* 44 (1982): 247–57.

Perry, William G. *Forms of Intellectual and Ethical Development in the College Years.* New York: Holt, 1970.

Peterson, Linda H. "Gender and the Autobiographical Essay: Research Perspectives, Pedagogical Practices. *College Composition and Communication* 42 (1991): 170–83.

Phelps, Louise Wetherbee. "Audience and Authorship: The Disappearing Boundary." *A Sense of Audience in Written Communication.* Ed. Gesa Kirsch and Duane Roen. Newbury Park, CA: Sage, 1990. 153–74.

Rafoth, Bennett. "Audience Adaptations in the Essays of Proficient and Nonproficient Freshman Writers." *Research in the Teaching of English* 19 (1985): 237–53.

Rice, Joy, and Annette Hemmings. "Women's Colleges and Women Achievers: An Update." *Signs: Journal of Women in Culture and Society* 13 (1988): 546–59.

Rich, Adrienne. Foreword. *Working it Out: 23 Women Writers, Artists, Scientists, and Scholars Talk about Their Lives and Work.* Ed. Sara Ruddick and Pamela Davis. New York: Pantheon, 1977. xiii–xxiv.

Richardson, Laurel. "Sharing Feminist Research with Popular Audiences: The Book Tour." *Beyond Methodology: Feminist Scholarship as Lived Research.* Ed. Mary Fonow and Judith Cook. Bloomington: Indiana UP, 1991. 284–95.

Ritchie, Joy. "Confronting the 'Essential' Problem: Reconnecting Feminist Theory and Pedagogy." *Journal of Advanced Composition* 10 (1990): 249–73.

————. Letter to the author. 29 May 1992.

Rose, Mike. *Lives on the Boundary.* New York: Penguin, 1989.

Roth, Robert. "The Evolving Audience: Alternatives to Audience Accommodation." *College Composition and Communication* 38 (1987): 47–55.

Russ, Joanna. *How to Suppress Women's Writing.* Austin: U of Texas P, 1983.

Sadker, Myra, and David Sadker. "Confronting Sexism in the College Classroom." *Gender in the Classroom: Power and Pedagogy.* Ed. Susan Gabriel and Isaiah Smithson. Urbana: U of Illinois P, 1990. 176–87.

Schor, Naomi. "This Essentialism Which Is Not One: Coming to Grips with Irigaray." *Differences: A Journal of Feminist Cultural Studies* 1 (1989): 38–58.

Schwager, Sally. "Educating Women in America." *Reconstructing the Academy: Women's Education and Women's Studies.* Ed. Elizabeth Minnich, Jean O'Barr, and Rachel Rosenfeld. Chicago: U of Chicago P, 1988. 154–93.

Schweickart, Patrocinio. "Reading, Teaching, and the Ethic of Care." *Gender in the Classroom: Power and Pedagogy.* Ed. Susan Gabriel and Isaiah Smithson. Urbana: U of Illinois P, 1990. 78–95.

Simeone, Angela. *Academic Women: Working Towards Equality.* South Hadley, MA: Bergin and Garvey, 1987.

Solomon, Barbara Miller. *In the Company of Educated Women: A History of Women and Higher Education in America.* New Haven: Yale UP, 1985.

Sommers, Nancy. "Between the Drafts." *College Composition and Communication* 43 (1992): 23–31.

Spelman, Elizabeth. *Inessential Woman: Problems of Exclusion in Feminist Thought.* Boston: Beacon, 1988.

Spender, Dale. "The Gatekeepers: A Feminist Critique of Academic Publishing." *Doing Feminist Research.* Ed. Helen Roberts. New York: Routledge, 1981. 186–202.

————. *Man Made Language.* 2d ed. New York: Routledge, 1980.

Spender, Dale, and Elizabeth Sarah, eds. *Learning to Lose: Sexism and Education.* London: Women's Press, 1980.

Spitzack, Carole, and Kathryn Carter. "Research on Women's Communication: The Politics of Theory and Method." *Doing Research on Women's Communication: Perspectives on Theory and Method.* Ed. Carter and Spitzack. Norwood, NJ: Ablex, 1989. 11–39.

Steinitz, Victoria, and Sandra Kantor. "Becoming Outspoken: Beyond Connected Education." *Women's Studies Quarterly* 19 (1991): 138–53.

Sullivan, Patricia A. "Feminism and Methodology in Composition Studies." *Methods and Methodology in Composition Research*. Ed. Gesa Kirsch and Sullivan. Carbondale: Southern Illinois UP, 1992. 37–61.

———. "Writing in the Graduate Curriculum: Literary Criticism as Composition." *Journal of Advanced Composition* 11 (1991): 283–99.

Tannen, Deborah. *You Just Don't Understand: Women and Men in Conversation*. New York: Morrow, 1990.

Tedesco, Janis. "Women's Ways of Knowing/Women's Ways of Composing." *Rhetoric Review* 9 (1991): 246–57.

Thibault, Gisele Marie. *The Dissenting Feminist Academy: A History of the Barriers to Feminist Scholarship*. New York: Lang, 1987.

Thomas, Lewis. *The Lives of a Cell: Notes of a Biology Watcher*. New York: Bantam, 1975.

Tidball, Elizabeth. "Women's Colleges and Women Achievers Revisited." *Signs: Journal of Women in Culture and Society* 5 (1980): 504–17.

Todd, Alexandra Dundas, and Sue Fisher. "Theories of Gender, Theories of Discourse." *Gender and Discourse: The Power of Talk*. Ed. Todd and Fisher. Norwood, NJ: Ablex, 1988. 1–16.

Tomlinson, Barbara. "Ong May Be Wrong: Negotiating with Nonfictional Readers." *A Sense of Audience in Written Communication*. Ed. Gesa Kirsch and Duane Roen. Newbury Park, CA: Sage, 1990. 85–98.

Tompkins, Jane. "Fighting Words: Unlearning to Write the Critical Essay." *Georgia Review* 42 (1988): 585–90.

———. "Me and My Shadow." *New Literary History* 19 (1987): 169–78.

Treichler, Paula A., Cheris Kramarae, and Beth Stafford, eds. *For Alma Mater: Theory and Practice in Feminist Scholarship*. Urbana: U of Illinois P, 1985.

Walzer, Arthur. "Articles from the 'California Divorce Project': A Case Study of the Concept of Audience." *College Composition and Communication* 36 (1985): 150–59.

Weedon, Chris. *Feminist Practice and Poststructuralist Theory*. Cambridge, MA: Blackwell, 1987.

Weiler, Kathleen. *Women Teaching for Change: Gender, Class, and Power*. New York: Bergin and Garvey, 1988.

Welch, Lynne, ed. *Women in Higher Education: Changes and Challenges*. New York, Praeger, 1990.

Wood, Julia T., and Charles Conrad. "Paradox in the Experiences of Professional Women." *The Western Journal of Speech Communication* 47 (1983): 305–22.

Woolf, Virginia. *A Room of One's Own.* New York: Harcourt, 1957.

Zawacki, Terry Myers. "Recomposing as a Woman—An Essay in Different Voices." *College Composition and Communication* 43 (1992): 32–38.

Gesa E. Kirsch is an assistant professor of English at Wayne State University in Detroit, Michigan, where she teaches courses in composition theory and women's studies. Her work has appeared in *Research in the Teaching of English, College English, Journal of Basic Writing*, and other journals. She is coeditor (with Duane Roen) of *A Sense of Audience in Written Communication* and (with Patricia A. Sullivan) of *Methods and Methodology in Composition Research*.